ISBN 978-1-331-97479-6
PIBN 10262927

This book is a reproduction of an important historical work. Forgotten Books uses
state-of-the-art technology to digitally reconstruct the work, preserving the original format
whilst repairing imperfections present in the aged copy. In rare cases, an imperfection in
the original, such as a blemish or missing page, may be replicated in our edition. We do,
however, repair the vast majority of imperfections successfully; any imperfections that
remain are intentionally left to preserve the state of such historical works.

1 MONTH OF
FREE
READING

at

www.ForgottenBooks.com

By purchasing this book you are eligible for one month membership to ForgottenBooks.com, giving you unlimited access to our entire collection of over 700,000 titles via our web site and mobile apps.

To claim your free month visit:

Similar Books Are Available from
www.forgottenbooks.com

INDUSTRIAL PUBLISHER,
406 WALNUT STREET,
1865.

INDUSTRIAL PUBLISHER,
406 WALNUT STREET,
1865.

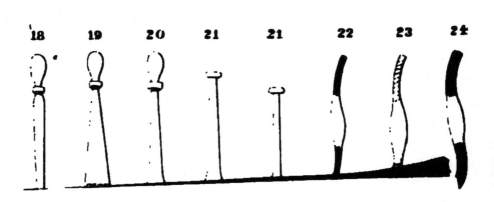

MARBLE-WORKERS' MANUAL.

DESIGNED FOR THE USE OF

MARBLE-WORKERS, BUILDERS,

AND

OWNERS OF HOUSES.

CONTAINING PRACTICAL INFORMATION RESPECTING MARBLES IN
GENERAL; THEIR CUTTING, WORKING, AND POLISHING;
VENEERING OF MARBLE; PAINTING UPON AND COLOR-
ING OF MARBLE; MOSAICS; COMPOSITION AND USE
OF ARTIFICIAL MARBLE, STUCCOS, CEMENTS:
RECEIPTS, SECRETS, ETC., ETC.

Translated from the French,

BY M. L. BOOTH.

WITH AN APPENDIX
CONCERNING AMERICAN MARBLES.

PHILADELPHIA:
HENRY CAREY BAIRD,
INDUSTRIAL PUBLISHER,
406 WALNUT STREET,
1865.

210220

PREFACE.

THE art of the Marble worker may be classed among those employments possessing the most interest and variety. It demands of its votary the knowledge of design, that of public and private monuments, and of the natural history of Marbles. It demands, also, taste and patience, without which the sculptor will be a bungler, instead of an artist. The cotemporary of civilization, his hand is found in the works of every century. The more greatness has belonged to nations, the more occasions had the artist to celebrate it ; and if the monuments of Greece and Rome had not been pillaged by the invasions of the barbarians, their sculptures would have borne witness to the flourishing state of the arts upon those two principal points of the globe.

Less ambitious at present, as great fortunes are rare, the artist must employ himself upon the ordinary wants of private life ; and if a few public monuments still demand his chisel, these are but exceptional, and in large cities. This is a misfortune, yet it is not without its compensations. These large fortunes, by their infinite subdivision, have given rise to that middle class, who, on their part, take delight in what they call conveniences, and demand of the Marble worker chimney-pieces, tables, vases, tombs, and funereal monuments, panelings, pavements more or less decorated with stone and Marble, and even fountains, flag and curbstones, frontings for the outside of warehouses, and counters, slabs and fixtures for interiors. In this respect the Marble workers of our times differ from those who only devoted themselves to churches and palaces. It is, therefore, important to place within the reach of skillful workmen the information and models which they need, and which are here extracted from the best authorities, in order to encourage and stimulate good taste.

The Manual of the Marble worker has been long demanded. It has also been needed by those proprietors who themselves desire to superintend works for which they do not choose to employ an architect. They will find in this manual all the information necessary to instruct them. We have probably invented nothing, but we have endeavored to make the most complete possible analysis of the treatises upon ancient and modern Marble working, which until now have only been found in folios so costly and bulky, that it was very difficult to consult, and almost impossible to possess them.

Our little volume, on the contrary, presenting a clear and precise text, and free from all the scientific phrases which perplex the subject, will be in the possession of every person who seeks information respecting the art of Marble working. It will be understood; it will excite comparative ideas; it will draw forth essays; it will attract attention to this art; and our object will be gained if it restores to the ateliers of the Marble workers some of the emulation which they seem to have lost.

It is divided into five parts.

The first treats of Marbles in general, of their qualities beauties, and defects.

PREFACE.

The second treats of the use, cutting, and polishing of the different Marbles which are in commerce.

The third describes the processes designed to facilitate and perfect the labor of the workman.

The fourth part is devoted to plated Marbles, stuccos, mosaic paintings, and terraces—the whole being the practical experience of the most skillful Marble workers.

The fifth part comprises new processes, secrets, recipes, an essay on the manufacture of toy marbles, and various other matters pertaining to the art.

We have also endeavored to enlighten the workmen respecting their true interests, and to warn them against the mistaken principles which sometimes mislead them, by pointing out the right course, and inspiring in them, as well as in us, that love of truth and commercial integrity, without which no industrial establishment will ever gain the confidence of the public or secure honorable profits.

TABLE OF CONTENTS.

	PAGE.
Alabaster	17
Appendix—Concerning American Marbles	243
Artificial Marble	158
" " , and Stuccos	119
Atelier of the Marble worker	115
Breccias, modern	80
Cement, universal	114
Chimney-piece in malachite	218
Chinese Paintings, unalterable	167
Coloring of Marbles	81
Coloring of Artificial Marbles	228
Crab, the	84
Crane, the	88
Defects of Marbles	82
Designs for the execution of works	215
Different varieties of Marbles	15
Figures in relief upon Marbles	227
Granite	45
Imitations of Marbles	119
Imitations of Mosaics	205
Jack-screw, the	89
Jasper	40

PAGE.

Lapis.. 16

Mastics.. 109
Mastics for cementing Marbles..................... 112
Masons' Mastic for Cisterns, etc.................. 118
Marbles in general................................. 11
Marble, ancient method for painting............... 221
Marble, Artificial................................. 153
Marble, Artificial, composition of................ 155
Marble, Artificial, coloring of................... 228
Marbles, coloring of............................... 81
Marbles, cleansing of.............................. 200
Marbles, cutting, working, and polishing of....... 50
Marbles, defects of................................ 82
Marbles, different varieties of.................... 15
Marbles, figures in relief upon.................... 227
Marbles, imitations of............................. 119
Marbles, modern.................................... 20
Marbles, machinery for raising..................... 91
Marbles, machinery for sawing and molding......... 102
Marbles, machinery for sculpturing or reducing.... 104
Marbles, manner of working......................... 55
Marbles, toy manufacture of........................ 192
Marble working, ornamental......................... 72
Marbles, painting upon............................. 140
Marble, turned..................................... 229
Marble, veneering of............................... 168
Marbles, workmanship of............................ 83
Mosaics.. 62
Mosaics by absorption.............................. 202
Mosaics, imitations of............................. 205

Ornamental Marble work............................. 72

PAGE.

Porphyries.. 16
Porphyries and Granites 89
Pozzolana.... 212
Pumice stone 213
Prefacc.... 8

Quartz... 89

Recipes, various.. 201

Sculptor, the.... 72
Sculpture by Acids.. 75
Serpentine. ....:. 16
Setting up of works 59
Slabs of Marble, composition of.... 160
Slabs, casting of.... 161
Slabs, tannage of. 163
Stuccos.... 120
Stuccos and Artificial Marbles 119
Stuccos, moldings in. 137
Stuccos, pictures in.... 228

Tackle, the.... 88
Terraces, Venetian 71
Terraces, preparation of area 173
Terraces, working of Marble for 178
Terraces, Venetian, less costly 188
Turned Marble 229

Universal Cement. 114

Veneering upon Marble.... 63
Veneering upon Wood and Stone 63
Vocabulary.... 232

Winch, the.... 86

First Part.

OF MARBLES IN GENERAL.

SECTION FIRST.

OF THE FORMATION, QUALITIES, BEAUTIES, AND DEFECTS OF MARBLE.

§ 1. MARBLE, according to every analysis which has been made of it, is a calcareous stone of different degrees of hardness, of a fine grain, often colored, and always susceptible of polish. As among other calcareous stones, there are Marbles of the first, second, and perhaps of the third formation. The old Marbles are not, like the new, composed of simple stony particles, reduced by the action of water into minute molecules; they are formed, like other ancient stones, of fragments of stones still more ancient, and the most of them are mixed with shells and other marine productions. All are deposited in horizontal beds, or parallelly inclined, and differ only in colors from other calcareous stones; for there are some stones which are almost as hard, as dense, and as fine grained as Marbles, to which, nevertheless, this name is not given, because they have no decided color, or rather, no diversity of colors.   These colors, although very deeply imprinted in certain Marbles, do not change their nature in other respects : they add nothing to their hardness or density, nor do they prevent their calcination and conversion into lime by the same degree of heat as with other hard stones.

Stones which are of a fine grain and susceptible of polish, form a link between the common stone and Marbles ; all are of the same nature, since all effervesce with acids, all break in granulated fragments, and all can be reduced to lime.

I say all, because I speak only here of pure Marbles, that is, of those composed entirely of calcareous matter, with no admixture of clay, slate, lava, or other vitreous materials ; those which are largely mixed with these heterogeneous substances are not true Marbles, but demi-stones, to be separately considered.

§ 2.   The beds of old Marble were formed, like other calcareous beds, from the deposit of the sea, small quantities of stony substances, shells, gravel, pebbles, &c., being washed together and stratified. The local establishment of most of these beds of Marble of ancient formation seems to have preceded that of other beds of calcareous stones, as they are almost always found beneath such beds, and, in a hill composed of twenty or thirty beds of stone, there are usually but two or three, often but one, of Marble ; these always lie beneath the others and near the clay which forms the base of the hill, either resting upon it, or only separated from it by another bed which seems to be the residuum of all the others, being made up of Marble, pyrites, and a large quantity of sparry crystallizations.

Thus, by their situation beneath the other beds of calcareous earth, these old Marbles have received the colors and petrifying fluids which the water always collects in its passage through the vegetable earth and the beds of stone which intervene between this and the Marble beds. These first formations of Marble are distinguished by several characteristics. Some bear the prints of finely marked shells; others, as the Lumachella, or fire-marble, seem composed of small snail-shaped shells; others contain belemnites, (1) fragments of madrepores, (2) &c. These Marbles bearing the imprints of shells are less common than the Breccias, which contain few marine products, but are made up of pebbles and rounded flints, joined with a stony cement, forming angular fragments when broken, whence this name. (3.)

§ 3. These Marbles of the first formation may be divided into two classes, the first comprising those

1. Belemnites—organic remains of extinct fossil bodies, with a straight, tapering shell.

2. Madrepores. Fossil-coral of the class of Zoophytes, consisting of carbonate of lime with a slight mixture of membraneous animal substance.

3. Breccia. From the French term "Breche," signifying notched or angular.

called Breccias, and the second, the Shell-marbles. Both contain veins of spar, yet they are more frequent and more apparent in the shell-marbles, than in the Breccias.   What the artisans call "*flaws*" in blocks of calcareous earth, are also small veins of spar, and the stone often breaks in the direction of these flaws while working it with the mallet; yet sometimes this spar acquires so much solidity, especially when mixed with combinations of iron, as to offer as much resistance as the other material.

§ 4.   The analysis of the substance of White Marble, and the sparry grains which are perceived on breaking it, seem to demonstrate that it was formed by the distillation of water.   It is also worthy of notice that, when worked, it yields equally to the mallet in every direction, whether cut horizontally or upright, while Marbles of the first formation can be worked horizontally with greater ease than in any other manner.   These colors can be easily perceived in the quarries, or on the rough-blocks.   Their immersion in water draws out the colors, and gives them for the moment, as much lustre as the highest polish.

§ 5.   There are but few Marbles, of much bulk at least, which are of a single color.   Some fine black and white specimens are the only ones which can be quoted, and even these are often tinged with grey or brown.   All others are of various colors.   It may, indeed, be said that every shade of color is visible in Marbles.   We have red with its various shades, orange yellow and yellowish, green and greenish, blues, more or less decided, and violet. These last two colors are the most rare, yet they are seen in the *Violet Breccia*, and in the *Bleuturquin*, a Marble obtained from Genoa and several other quarries, and particularly suited to furniture and chimney pieces. From the mingling of these colors result an infinitude of shades in the grey, dove, whitish, brown, and blackish Marbles.

§ 6. The natural brilliancy and intensity of the colors of Marble can be increased by art. For this end it is only necessary to heat them. The red will become more vivid, and the yellow will change into an orange or vermilion. The heat necessary to work this change is acquired by polishing them till hot, and the shades of color brought out in this simple manner are permanent, and remain unchanged by cold or time; they are durable because deeply imprinted, and the entire mass of Marble would receive this increase of colors by an intense heat.

§ 7. The ground, which is generally of a uniform color, should be distinguished from those parts which are stained or veined, often with different colors; these veins traverse the bottom, and are rarely intersected by others, they being of a later formation than the bottom, and only filling crevices caused by the waste of the first material. In the same manner, the stains are rarely traversed by other stains unless by a few threads of herborizations of a still later formation,

and it should be remarked that these stains termi-
nate irregularly, with broken edges, while the veins
are neither indented or broken, and are usually distinctly marked through their course.

It often happens that portions differently colored,
and differently marked with spots and veins, are found
in the same quarries, and sometimes in the same block;
yet in general, the marbles of a country resemble each
other more strongly than those foreign to them. This
peculiarity they have in common with other calcareous
stones which are of the same texture and of different
grains.

§ 8. There are some rough Marbles which are
worked with difficulty, resisting the tools of the workmen, and often breaking into splinters. Some others
of a softer nature crumble instead of splintering.
Many others are filled with cavities; some are traversed by numerous threads of a tender spar, and are
called by the workmen Stringy Marbles.

§ 9. The Italian Marbles are very numerous, and
are more celebrated than any European Marbles. That
of Carrara, which is white, is taken from the coasts
of Genoa in blocks of an unlimited size. It has a
crystalline grain, and is comparable in purity to the
ancient Marble of Paros.

The Marble of Saravezza, which is found in the
same mountains as that of Carrara, is of a still finer
grain; a red and white Marble is also found there,
with red and white spots distinctly marked; this Mar-

ble resembles a Breccia, and is called Brocatello; a blackish tint is also sometimes seen in it. Its quarry is almost as continuous as that of Carrara, and of all other white or colored crystalline Marbles found in Sienna, or in the Genoese territories; all of these are found in large masses, in which no indication of shells is to be seen; a few crevices are there, filled up by a crystallization of calcareous spar. No doubt all these Marbles are of second formation.

The environs of Carrara also furnish two kinds of Green Marble; one, incorrectly termed *Egyptian Green*, is of a deep green, with white and flaxen grey spots; the other, called *Sea Green*, is of a clearer color, veined with white.

§ 10. The White Marble of Paros is the most re nowned of antique Marbles. The great artists of Greece employed it in those exquisite statues which we still admire, not only for the perfection of the workmanship, but also for their preservation during more than twenty centuries. This Marble is found in the isles of Paros, Naxos, and Tinos. Its grain is coarser than that of Carrara, and it is mixed with a great quantity of small crystals of spar; these cause it to crumble easily while working, and it is also these which give it almost as great a degree of transpa- rency as alabaster, which it resembles in softness.

§ 11. In Spain, as well as in Italy and Greece, there are hills, entire mountains even, of White Mar- ble. A kind is also found in the Pyrennes, on the side of the Bayonne, which is similar to the Marble of Carrara, with the exception of the grain, which is coarser, and which gives it a strong resemblance to the white Parian Marble; but it is softer than the last, and its white often takes a yellowish tinge. Another Marble of greenish-brown, spotted with red, is also found in the same mountains.

In the suburbs of Molina, a flesh-colored and white Marble is found, and about a quarter of a league from there, others, red, yellowish, and black, and grained like that of Carrara, but these quarries are quite scarce.

§ 12. The marble called *Antique Breccia* seems a sort of calcareous pudding-stone, composed of large pieces distinctly rounded, some of which are white, blue and red, and others black. This variety of colors gives a beautiful appearance to this Marble. The Breccia of Aleppo is also composed of rounded pieces of a dove-color. The Breccia of Saravezzia presents rounded fragments of a very large size, the most of which are violet; the others white or yellowish.

All the calcareous pudding-stones are varieties of Breccias, and no distinction would have been made between them, did they not usually differ in their cement, which is softer, and unsusceptible of polish. Only one more degree of petrifaction is needed to make them perfectly similar to the finest Breccias, as the cement of those pudding-stones composed of vitreous flints needs but one shade of petrefaction to be converted into a material as hard as porphyry or jasper.

SECTION SECOND.

DIFFEFENT VARIETIES OF MARBLE.

MARBLE, according to most authorities, is an extremely hard species of rock, bearing the name of the country in which are the quarries where it is obtained; sometimes, also, of the mountains from whence it is taken; as the Vosgean and Pyrenean Marbles.—Marble is antique or modern.

The antique Marbles comprise those of which the quarries have been exhausted, and which are only known to us through the works of the ancients.

The modern Marbles are those which we now use, and the quarries of which are still in existence. It is generally used for casings or inlaying; rarely in the block on account of its high price, unless for vases, statues, columns and other works of this kind. Many fine examples exist of interior and exterior decoration.

Although the varieties of Marble are infinite, they are reduced to two species, the veined and the Breccian, the latter being simply a mass of small stones firmly knit together in such a manner that, when broken, they form angles, whence their name.

OF THE ANTIQUE MARBLES.

§ 13. The antique Marble, the quarries of which were in Greece, and from which were the beautiful statues still existing in Italy, is absolutely unknown at present. In its stead we use that of Carrara.

The Lapis is regarded as the finest of the antique Marbles. It is of a deep blue color, stained with a clearer sky blue, and intermixed with veins of gold. On account of its rarity, this was only used for inlaying; several specimens of it in Mosaic may still be seen in slabs in castles.

§ 14. Porphyry passes for the hardest of the antique Marbles, and, after the Lapis, one of the finest; it was formerly brought from Numidia in Africa, for which reason it was called by the ancients the Numidian Lapis. It is red, green, and grey. The red porphyry is very hard, of a deep red color, approaching wine lees, and studded with small white spots. It is very susceptible of polish. The largest specimen of it in France is the laver of king Dagobert. The finest is that of the deepest red, with the whitest and smallest spots. The green porphyry, which is much rarer, has the same hardness. It is mixed with small green spots and grey points. A few slabs and vases of it still exist. The grey porphyry is spotted with black, and is much softer.

The Serpentine, thus called by the ancients from

the resemblance of its color to that of the serpent. was formerly obtained from the Egyptian quarries. This Marble possesses much of the hardness of porphyry. Its color is of a greenish brown, mixed with a few square and round pale green spots and yellow veins. Its rarity caused it only to be used in Mosaic.

OF ALABASTER.

§15. Alabaster is a species of Marble either white and transparent, or variegated with several colors, and is taken from the Alps and the Pyrenees. It is very soft when first taken from the quarry, but hardens much on exposure to the air. There are several varieties—the white, the variegated, the montahuto, the violet, and the roquebrue. The white alabaster is used for vases, statues, and other objects of a medium size. The variegated is divided into three kinds: the Oriental, the Floral, and the Agate. There are two varieties of the Oriental; the first in the form of an Agate, the second mixed with red, blue, yellow, and white veins. The Floral alabaster is of two kinds · one spotted with various colors resembling flowers, whence its name—the other, veined like the Agate cold and transparent. The Agate alabaster is similar to the Oriental, but has paler colors. The alabaster of Montahuto is very soft, yet harder than the German Agate, which it strongly resembles.— The ground is brown, traversed by grey veins, somewhat in the style of geographical charts.

OF GRANITE.

§ 16. Granite, thus called because marked with small dots formed of several grains of condensed gravel, is very hard, and takes polish badly. It is evident that no other Marble was used by the ancients in large quantities, since most of the edifices of Rome, even to the dwellings of private citizens, were decorated with it. Doubtless this Marble was abundant, from the numerous shafts of columns which even now serve as boundaries in every quarter of the city. There are many varieties; the Italian, the Egyptian, and that of Dauphiny—the green, and the violet. The Egyptian granite, known as the *Thebaïcum marmor*, and taken from the Desert of Thebaïd, has a dirty white ground, mixed with small grey and greenish spots, and is almost as hard as porphyry. The granite of Dauphiny, found on the banks of the Rhone, near the mouth of the Iser, is very ancient, as appears from some columns which are in Provence. The green granite is a kind of Serpentine, or antique green, mixed with little green and white spots; several columns of this kind of marble are to be seen at Rome. The violet granite, brought from the Egyptian quarries, is dotted with small spots of white and violet.— The most of the antique obelisks of Rome are of this Marble, such as that of Saint Peter of the Vatican, Saint John of Latran, the People's Gate, and others.

§ 17. The Marble of Jasper is of a greenish color, with small red spots. There is another antique jasper, which is black and white, with small spots. This is very rare.

The green antique Marble is also very rare. Its color is a mixture of grass and dark green, with spots of different form and size.

The black and white Marbles, the quarries of which are lost, are made up of slabs of the purest white and the deepest black.

The little antique Marble is of this last variety, but more covered with small veins, resembling the Barbançon Marble.

§ 18. The Brocatello Marble was formerly found near Adrianople. Its color is a mixture of grey, red, light, yellow, and dove tints.

The African Marble is spotted with reddish brown, mingled with veins of a dirty white and flesh color, with a few threads of a deep green.

The black antique Marble was of two kinds; one called *marmor lucullum*, brought from Greece, was very soft. It was of this Marble that Marcus Scaurus caused the columns, thirty-eight feet in height, with which his palace was decorated, to be sculptured.

The yellow Marble has two varieties. One, called Sienna yellow, is of a yellowish dove color, without veins, and very rare, and was only used for Mosaic work in panels; the other, called golden, and yellower than the first, is that to which Pausanius gave the name of *marmor croceum*, because of its saffron color.   It was found near Macedonia.

§ 19. The Lumachella marble, thus called because it is a mixture of white, grey, and black spots, in the form of snail-shaped shells, is very rare, the quarries being lost.

————

SECTION THIRD.

OF MODERN MARBLES.

§ 20. The white Marble which is now taken from Carrara, near the shores of Genoa, is hard and very white, and is suitable for bas-reliefs and other works of sculpture.   Blocks of any size can be obtained; hard crystals are also found there.

That Marble of Carrara termed Virgin Marble is white, and is taken from the Pyrenees, on the side of Bayonne.   It is finer grained than the last, glitters like a species of salt, and resembles the white antique Marble from which the Grecian statues were made, but is softer, not as fine, and is apt to grow yellow and to spot.   This kind is used in sculpture.

The modern black Marble is pure and spotless, like the antique, and is much harder.

The Dinan Marble, which is obtained near the city of that name, in the country of Liege, is very abundant, and of a pure and fine black. It is used for monuments, and especially for pavements.

The Marble of Namur is also very abundant, and as black as that of Dinan, but not as perfect. It has a slight bluish tinge, and is traversed by a few greyish veins. In Holland a great traffic is made of its tiles.

The Marble of Theé, which is found in the country of Liege, is entirely black, soft, and easily worked, and is susceptible of a higher polish than those of Namur and Dinan. It is, therefore, especially suitable for monumental use.

The white-veined Marble which comes from Carrara, is of a deep blue on a white ground, mixed with grey spots and small veins. This Marble is apt to spot and grow yellow; it is used for pedestals and entablatures.

The Marble of Margoire, which is brought from Milan, is very hard, and quite abundant. Its color is a blue ground, mixed with brown veins of the color of iron. A part of the dome of Milan is built of it.

The black and white Marble which is taken from the abbey of Leff, near Dinan, has a deep black ground with very white veins.

The Barbançon Marble, found in the country of Hainaut, is black, veined with white and is abundant.

The shafts of the six composite columns of the canopy of *Val de Grace* are of this Marble.

The Givet Marble is procured near Charlemont, on the frontiers of the Luxembourg. It is black, veined with white, but more sparsely than that of Barbançon.

The Portor Marble is taken from the foot of the Alps, in the suburbs of Carrara. There are two varieties of it; the finest has a deep black ground mingled with spots and golden yellow veins; the other, with whitish veins, is less esteemed.

The Marble of Saint Maximin is a species of Portor, the yellow and black being more vivid.

The modern Serpentine Marble comes from Germany, and is more used for vases and similar ornaments than for works of architecture.

§ 21. The modern Green Marble is of two kinds; one, improperly called *Egyptian Green*, is found near Carrara, on the coast of Genoa. Its color is deep green, with a few white and flaxen grey spots; the other, which is called *Sea Green*, is of a brighter green, and veined.

The parti-colored Marble resembles the antique jasper; the finest is that which resembles it the most closely.

§ 22. The modern Lumachello Marble comes from Italy, and strongly resembles the antique, but the spots are not as distinctly marked.

The Brema Marble, also found in Italy, has a yellow ground mixed with white spots.

The Peacock-eye Marble is also brought from Italy, and is mixed with white, bluish, and red spots, somewhat resembling the sort of eyes in the feathers of the peacock, whence its name.

The Serena Marble is mixed with large spots, and grey, yellow, and reddish veins.

The Peach-blossom Marble, which is found in Italy, has white, red, and a few yellow spots.

The Marble *di Vescovi*, or Bishop's Marble, also found in Italy, has greenish veins, crossed by white bands—long, round, and transparent.

§ 23.   The Brocatello Marble, called Spanish Brocatello, which is taken from an antique quarry of Tortosa, in Andalusia, is very rare.   Its color is a mixture of yellow, red, grey, pale and dove tints.

The Boulogne Marble is a kind of Brocatello which is found in Picardy, but with larger spots, mixed with a few red threads.

The Champagne Marble, resembling the Brocatello, is mixed with blue in round spots, like the eyes of a partridge; it is sometimes found shaded with white and pale yellow tints.

§ 24.   The Marble of Saint Baume is brought from that part of Provence, and is of a red and white ground, mixed with yellow, and similar to the Brocatello.

The Marble of Tray, found in the neighborhood of

the preceding, closely resembles it. It has a yellowish ground, slightly spotted with red, and shaded with grey and white.

§ 25. The Languedoc Marble has two varieties. One kind, found near the city of Cosne, in Languedoc, is very abundant. It has a dirty, vermilion-red ground, intermixed with large veins and white spots. It is used for decorations of court-yards, peristyles, archways, &c.

The Griotte Marble, so called from its resemblance to griottes, or cherries, is also taken from near Cosne, and has a deep red ground, mingled with dirty white.

§ 26. The Marble called *Bleuturquin*, comes from the coast of Genoa. It is of a blue ground, mixed with dirty white; it is apt to grow yellow, and it spots easily; but the casings, consoles, and hearths which are made of it are so generally used, that it has long been in vogue, and its price sustained, despite the defects of which we have spoken.

§ 27. The Serancolin was obtained from a spot called the Golden Valley, near Serancolin. It is of a blood color, mixed with grey, yellow, and some transparent spots, like the agate; the finest is very rare, the quarry being exhausted. A few specimens of it still exist in ancient castles.

§ 28. The Campan is taken from quarries near Tarbes; there are white, red, green, and dove-color varieties, veined and spotted. The Green Campan is of a bright green, mixed only with white, and is very common. It is used for casings, tables, hearths, etc.

The Signan Marble is of a greenish brown, with red, or flesh-colored and grey spots, and a few green threads; it resembles the green Campan.

The Marble of Savoy, brought from that country, has a red ground mixed with several other colors which seem to be cemented.

The Gauchenet Marble, procured near Dinan, is of a red-white ground, spotted, and mixed with a few white veins.

The Marble of Leff, an abbey near Dinan, is of a pale red, with large stains and a few white veins. The capital of the chancel behind the canopy of the *Val-de-Grace*, at Paris, is of this Marble.

§ 29. The Marble of Rance, from the country of Hainaut, is very abundant. It has a dirty red ground, spotted, with blue and white veins. The principal specimens of it in Paris are the six Corinthian columns of the high altar in the Church of the Sorbonne.

§ 30. The Bourbon Marble, brought from that province, is of a bluish grey and dirty red, with veins of dirty yellow. It is generally used in compartments of pavements of saloons, vestibules, peristyles, etc.

§ 31. The Sicilian Marble is of two kinds, the ancient and the modern. The first is of a reddish brown, white and dove, with square and long spots, resembling striped taffeta; its colors are very vivid.

The Swiss Marble has a slate blue ground mixed with whitish tints.

OF MARBLES AND MODERN BRECCIAS.

§ 32. The White Breccia is a mixture of brown, grey and violet with large white spots.

The black, or Little Breccia, is of a grey or brown ground, mixed with black spots and little white dots, which produce but little effect.

The Golden Breccia is a mixture of yellow and white stains.

The Coraline Breccia has a few stains of a coral color.

The Violet, or modern Italian Breccia, has a reddish brown ground, with long violet veins or spots, mixed with white.

This Marble is beautiful in decorations of summer-houses, but if care is not taken of it, it loses its brilliant colors, and turns yellow. It is easily spotted by grease, wax, paint, oil, etc.

The dove-colored Breccia is a mixture of white, violet, and light spots, with large dove-colored stains This is the Marble used for boudoirs.

The Marble of the Pyrenees has a brown ground, mixed with grey, and several other colors.

The rough Breccia—so called because it contains all the colors of the other Breccias—is a mixture of red, grey, blue, white, and black spots.

The Verona Breccia is intermingled with blue, pale red, and crimson.

The Sauveterre Breccia is a mixture of black, grey, and yellow spots.

The Saravezzian Breccia has a brown and, violet ground, mixed with large white and dove spots.

The little Saravezzian Breccia is called thus, only because its spots are smaller than the preceding. ˙

ON THE COLORING OF MARBLES.

§ 33. By an easy process, different colors are given to Marbles. Colors extracted from vegetables, such as saffron, Brazilian wood, cochineal, litmus, dragon's blood, etc., when joined with a suitable dissolvent, as spirits of wine, urine mixed with quick lime and soda, oils, etc., stain the Marble, and penetrate it quite deeply; but to give it stronger, more durable and penetrating colors, metallic acidulous solutions are necessary, such as aqua-fortis, spirits of salts, etc.

Artificial marble can also be made. This process is commenced by making a foundation of plaster, tempered with glue water. This foundation is covered about half an inch in thickness with the following composition :

Take foliated and transparent plaster-stone, calcine it by fire, and reduce it to a very fine powder, dilute it with strong glue-water, and add red or yellow ochre, or whatever other color may be wished. The coloring should not be wholly mixed with the composition when veined Marble is desired. After this composition has been applied, and is perfectly dry, polish it by first rubbing it with fine sand, and afterwards with pumice, or tripoli stone, and finish by rubbing finally with oil.

§34. No particular description has ever been given of the fine Marbles of the Vosges mountains. There are two varieties; the granite with red tints, and the Marbles, black, grey, and shaded with dove and rose colors. The black has a few dirty white stains; its black has a reddish cast, which somewhat detracts from its beauty. The red is striped in straight lines upon a dove ground; the grey is almost a Breccia with points, or little brown, grey, or russet shell work. These varieties are easily worked, which fact has caused the establishment of several workshops at Epinal, where a large number of tables, slabs for bureaus and secretaries, etc., are fabricated, and many smaller articles are made by the prisoners, who are thus relieved, by occupation, from the dangers of idleness.

OF THE DEFECTS OF MARBLE.

§35. Marble, like stone, has faults which will cause its rejection by the merchant who is a judge of it. They are as follows :

Stubborn Marble is that which, on account of its excessive hardness, is very difficult to work, and is apt to fly off in splinters. This is the case with most hard Marbles.

Crumbly Marble is of the nature of sandstone, and when worked, cannot retain its sharp arris; the white Grecian Marble, that of the Pyrenees, and several others, are of this nature.

The Terraced Marble has soft spots in it called *terraces*, which it is often necessary to fill up with mastic. The Marble of Languedoc and Hon, and many of the Breccias, are examples of this class.

The Stringy Marble is crossed by flaws; as that of Saint Baume, Serancolin, Rance, and almost all colored Marbles.

The camlet Marble is that which, retaining the same color after polishing, appears tabbied; as that of Namur and some others.

OF MARBLE ACCORDING TO ITS WORKMANSHIP.

§ 36. Rough Marble is that which, having been taken from the quarry in specimen blocks, or for block works, remains unworked.

Rough hewn Marble is that which is cut in the yard with the saw, or simply squared with the mallet, according to the design of the vase, statue, profile, or other work of this kind.

Outlined Marble is that which, having received a few subordinate strokes for architecture or sculpture, is worked with the double point for one and the chisel for the other.

Pierced Marble is worked with the edge of the mallet to detach the front from the back part on the outside of works of a rustic order.

Polished Marble is that which, having been rubbed first with sandstone and the beater, and afterwards with pumice stone, is polished by hand with a linen cushion and emery dust for colored, and the powder of calcined tin for white Marbles, the emery being apt to redden them. In Italy a piece of lead is used instead of linen, which is better, and imparts a finer and more durable polish to the Marble; however, this costs much more time and pains.

Soiled, tarnished, or stained Marble can be repolished in the same manner. Spots of oil, especially upon white Marble, cannot be effaced, as they penetrate it.

Lump Marble is rubbed with shave grass or the skin of the sea-dog, to give a polished surface to the subordinate parts of sculpture or architecture.

Finished Marble is that which, having received all necessary work from the hand of the artisan, is ready for its place.

§ 37. Artificial Marble is manufactured from a composition of gypsum resembling stucco, in which different colors are mixed in imitation of Marble. This composition is tolerably hard, and takes polish, but is apt to chip off. Other artificial Marbles are also made by means of corrosive tinctures upon white Marble, which penetrates the surface about one-third of an inch; in this manner any kind of ornamental figures can be made, and the appearance of the most minutely carved foliation given to the Marble.

§ 38. Counterfeit Marble is painting which imi tates the colors, veins, and chance beauties of Marbles, and to which is given, by means of a varnish, an appearance of polish on wood or stone.

§ 39. We do not know how to better conclude these remarks than by an extract from M. Huot, who has reduced the Marble question to those which are practically best known in commerce, which is, after all, the point most interesting to Artists and Merchants.

Mineralogists, he says, divide Marbles into two great classes; the *calcaires saccharoides*, that is, those which break like sugar, and are most suitable to statuary; and the *calcaires sublamellaires*, which, from the fineness of their grain, are particularly suited to the decoration of buildings.

These are separated into two groups, the antique and the modern.

The following are the principal varieties:—The *Red Antique* was taken from the Egyptian quarries, situated between the Nile and the Red Sea. The chain of Taygetus, in Laconia, also furnished it, but of an inferior quality.

The *Black Antique*, or Lucullus Marble, is remarkable for its intensity of color. It is supposed to have been brought from Greece. Quarries of this Marble were also found near Spa, but they have long been abandoned.

The *Green Antique* is a Breccia, composed of fragments of serpentine and saccharoide Marbles, joined together with a calcareous cement. This was used in ,Thessalonica and Macedon.

The *Yellow Antique* was also found in Macedonia. It was from this Marble that the columns, composed of a single piece, which decorate the interior of the Pantheon, were made.

The *Violet Antique Breccia*, or Aleppian Breccia, was probably taken from Carrara, where some of it is still found. It is of various colors, and contains angular fragments of white and lilac limestone, joined with a violet cement.

The *African Antique Breccia*, composed of grey, red, and violet fragments, joined by a black, calcareous paste, is not less variegated than the preceding. This Marble produces a beautiful effect.

§ 40. Asia, Africa, America, Oceanica, Sweden, Norway, and Germany possess Marble quarries which, although less known than those of Italy and Greece, are neither inferior or less beautiful. But only in Italy can be found the *Sienna Yellow*, the *Florence Green*, the *Prato*, the *Bergamo*, the *Suza*, and the *Lumachella of Abruzzi*, or the *Statuary of Carrara* from the Genoese coasts, or the superb *Blcuturquin*, or *Bardiglio*, also taken from the suburbs of Carrara;

or the *Black Portor*, furrowed with numerous veins of a reddish yellow.

§ 41. Spain alone can rival Italy in Marbles. Her Marbles of Molina are considered as fine grained as those of Carrara. The provinces of Granada and Cordova possess those which equal them in purity. The *Grey* of Toledo, the *Black* of La Mancha, and of Biscay, the *Black, veined with White*, of Murviedro, the *Violet* of Catalonia, the *Red* of Seville and of Molina, the *Green* of Granada, the *Red* of Santiago, the red *Lumachellas* of Granada and Cordova, and the *Spanish Brocatellos* with yellow cement, form a collection of mineral riches, which only need skillful workmen to embellish both public and private edifices with all the splendor and prodigality of decorations of the artists of Greece and Rome.

§ 42. England also possesses fine quarries, which might rival those of the continent. The expense of transportation hinders the introduction of the English Marbles into France. They are seldom seen there except in museums.

§ 43. Belgium has considerable commerce in Marbles, especially in the kind called *Drap Mortuaire*, on which the white shells stand out distinctly from the black ground. It also has well known Marbles which are in great demand among workmen since the introduction of railways has facilitated their transport. Among these is the Granitel, a species of black Lumachella, interspersed with fragments of coral and other polypi, and found principally at Ligny and near Mons. The Saint Anne is also found there, and is of a grey ground with irregular white spots, or of a reddish grey ground with long and large white veins.

§ 44. But France can also compete, in her varied products, with those countries most favored by nature; she has grey, brown, ash and red Granites, whose beauty is equalled by their solidity. Those of Cherbourg, Boulogne, and the Vosges, unite these qualities.

All these Marbles, and many others which are still buried beneath beds of calcareous earth, long remained neglected or unknown on account of the expense of quarrying and transportation; perhaps, also, for the reason, too common in France, that we value less the products of our own soil than those of foreign countries; yet all these Marbles, we confidently assert, can compete advantageously with those of Italy or Greece.

The mechanical means now used for the quarrying of Marbles, the use of steam engines in cutting, working, and transporting them, and the diminution of their market price, will place them within reach of the world, and ere long we shall see them in baths, bases of columns, stairways, and garden vases and fountains, as substitutes for the stone which grows yellow, scales off, and is covered with disagreeable lichens and mosses, and the plaster which must often be replaced to the detriment of the owner.

But it is not private individuals alone who should modify the general ideas respecting Marble. It is most necessary that the Marble workers themselves, should endeavor to manufacture the small articles which are demanded in trade, at reasonable prices. It is a wrong system to put a high price on novelties. It is better, on the contrary, to make them popular; and the best means of accomplishing this is to offer them at a cheap rate. A new art of veneering Marble upon wood or stone, of which we shall speak hereafter, will favor the introduction of fine French Marbles in commerce. This veneering will be found very beautiful for mantels, consoles, tables, and other articles of the same nature, which are executed in Marble.

SECTION FOURTH.

OF PORPHYRIES AND GRANITES.

BEFORE occupying ourselves with these costly stones, we will say a few words respecting the primitive material which enters into their composition.

OF QUARTZ.

§ 45. Quartz is the first of the primitive glasses.—

This same material is supposed to form the great internal rock of the globe; its exterior portions, which form the base and nucleus of the highest elevations of the earth, are composed of the same primitive matter. The nucleus of these mountains became at first surrounded with, and covered by broken fragments of this glass, together with scales of jasper, spangles of mica, and little crystallized masses of feld-spar and shorl, from which were formed, by their union, huge masses of granite, porphyry, and all other vitreous rocks.

To perfectly understand the nature and formation of porphyry and granite, we must first define the difference between quartz and jasper.

OF JASPER.

§ 46. Jasper is simply a quartz, more or less filled with metallic particles; these color it, and render its fracture less clear than that of quartz; it is also more opaque. Yet as jasper, with the exception of its color, is only composed of a single substance, it may be regarded as a species of quartz, unmixed with anything but metallic vapors.

§ 47. Mica is a material, the substance of which is nearly as simple as that of quartz or jasper, and all three are of the same nature. Its formation is contemporary with that of these two glasses. It is not found, like them, in large, hard, and solid masses, but generally in spangles or small thin plates, and disseminated through other vitreous substances.. These spangles of mica have finally formed talcs, which are of the same nature, but with larger laminæ talcs or plates. Usually, small parcels of matter come from those which are in larger masses. Here, on the contrary, the large volume of talc is formed from particles of mica which first existed, and the molecules of which, being united by means of water, have formed talc in the same manner as sandstone is produced by the blending of quartzose sand.

§ 48. Common Talc is a kind of unctuous stone, soft, clean, pearl-colored, and easily separated into plates, which, when thin, are quite transparent. It is easily bent or cut, is greasy and fatty to the touch, is broken with difficulty, will bear a strong heat without suffering much change, and is not dissolved by any acid or alkaline menstruum in a liquid form. The most esteemed talc is that which is as transparent as clear water; that with a green tint is not as valuable.

Talc is prepared for commerce by splitting it into plates with a thin, two-edged knife, so that the back of the plate may not chip off. This is used throughout Siberia for windows and lanterns instead of glass, and no glass is clearer or more transparent than good talc.

Some talcs are greenish, yellow, and even black, and these colors, which affect their transparency, do not change their other qualities; these colored talcs are nearly as soft to the touch, and pliant to the hand,

and resist, like the white talc, the action of acids and fire.

It is easy to understand, from these facts respecting the composition of porphyry and granite, why they have a greater hardness and solidity than Marble; yet these are not the only materials which have aided in their foundation.

§ 49. Feld-spar is also a vitreous matter, and is sparry when broken; it is never found in large masses like quartz or jasper, but in small crystals incorporated in granite and porphyry; sometimes, also, in little isolated pieces in the purest clay, or in the sands formed from the decomposition of porphyry or granite, it being one of the constituent parts of these rocks. It is usually found crystallized and colored, and in small masses.

Feld-spar is sometimes opaque, like quartz, but oftener almost transparent. The different tints of red or violet with which its crystals are often colored, indicate a strong proximity between the time of its formation and that of the metallic sublimations which have penetrated and tinged jaspers of different colors.

§ 50. Shorl is the last of the five primitive glasses, and, as it has several characteristics in common with the feld-spar, it can be plainly seen, by contrasting them, that both have a common origin, and that both were formed at the same time, and by the same law of nature, during the general vitrification.

Shorl is a sparry glass—that is, composed of longitudinal *plates* like the feld-spar; it is also found in small crystallized masses, its crystals forming prisms surmounting pyramids.

This explained, we are naturally led to speak of porphyry. Quartz, jasper, mica, feld-spar, and shorl are, as we have just seen, the simplest substances which nature has produced by means of fire. We will now follow the combinations she has made by the mixture of two, three, four, and sometimes by the whole five together, to compose other substances by the same means of fire, at the time of the first consolidation of our globe. This seems to be a digression from our subject, but it is that we may penetrate it more deeply, and to initiate the Marble workers into this branch of the art, which is usually but little understood by them.

§ 51. Porphyry is the most precious of these composite substances, and, after the jasper, the most beautiful of all vitreous matter found in large masses. It is, as we have just said, composed of jasper, feld-spar, and small particles of shorl, mingled together. It cannot be confounded with the jaspers, they being of a simple substance, containing neither feld-spar or shorl; nor can it be classed with the granites, as they never contain jasper, but are made up of three or four other substances, namely, quartz, feld-spar, shorl, and mica.

The name of porphyry seems exclusively to designate a purplish red substance, which is, in fact, the color of the finest porphyry; but this title is extended to all porphyries, without distinction of color.

The red porphyry is interspersed with very small spots, more or less white, sometimes reddish. These spots are the particles of feld-spar and shorl which were disseminated and incorporated in the paste of the jasper. The essential characteristics of all porphyries, and by means of which they can always be recognized, is this mixture of feld-spar or shorl, or of both together, with the substance of the jasper; they are more opaque and highly colored when jasper enters largely in their composition, and become somewhat transparent by the presence of a larger quantity of feld-spar. The less opaque the porphyry, the harder it is, while, on the contrary, the more transparent the Marble, the softer is it found to be.

In porphyry the ground or paste is deeply colored; the grains of feld-spar and shorl are white, or sometimes of the color of the ground, but of a much paler shade; in granite, on the contrary, the feld-spar and shorl are colored,—and the quartz, which may be regarded as the paste, is always white. This proves that the substance of jasper is the base of porphyry, as quartz is that of granite.

§ 52. Although much less common than granite, porphyry is often found in masses, and in some places in large blocks. It is usually a neighbor of the jasper, and both rest, like the granite, upon quartzose rocks; this proximity indicates a contemporary formation.

The durable solidity of the substance of porphyry also proves its affinity with the jasper—neither tarnish, except by a long-continued action of watery elements, and of all substances in the world used in large quantities, quartz, jasper, and porphyry are the most unchangeable.

Black porphyry, properly called, has an entirely black ground, with small, oblong spots, and only differs from the red porphyry in color.

There is a porphyry with a brown ground, with large, greenish, oblong spots; another is also found with a reddish brown ground, with spots of bright green, and others of a blackish brown ground, with spots of blackish and greenish tints.

The green porphyry has several varieties; the green antique Serpentine, the ground of which is green, and the spots oblong or parallelopipedon, is of a bright or pale green, and partaking of the nature of feld-spar or shorl.

We will now pass to the second part of this section, which, though offering less interest to our curiosity, possesses for us a much greater degree of utility.

OF GRANITES.

§ 53. Of all matter produced by the primitive fire, granite is the least simple and the most varied; it is usually composed of quartz, feld-spar, and schorl, quartz, feld-spar, and mica, or of quartz, feld-spar, shorl, and mica.

The red tints of feld-spar and the blackish brown of shorl are, doubtless, attributable to the metallic sublimations, which, in the same manner, have colored the jasper, and which permeated the matter of feld-spar and shorl when in a state of fusion. However, all are not thus colored, as white and whitish feld-spars and shorls are found ; and in several kinds of granite and porphyry, feld-spar is not distinguishable from quartz by its color.

The Vosges, though not the highest elevations, are composed of granite, exhibiting no vestige of marine products, and these granites are not covered with cal-careous beds, although the sea has borne its relics to much greater heights in other places. With this ex-ception, it is only in high vitreous mountains that the ancient structure and primitive composition of the earth can be seen bare in masses of quartz, veins of jasper, groups of granite, and metallic veins.

When the metallic exhalations are abundant, and also mixed with other corrosive elements, they deteri orate the substance of the granite in time, and even change that of quartz : this is seen in the sides of all perpendicular clefts in which veins of metallic mines have been found—the quartz seems decomposed, and the adjacent granite is crumbly.

Buffon says, with reason, that granite is only found on high mountains, or at the foot of them, having been precipitated by time, or detached by waters. An important historical fact supports this theory; the discovery in a marsh of the piece of granite which serves for the base of the colossal statue of Peter the Great. This fragment belonged to no mass, and the neighboring mountain was surmounted by pieces of the same nature.

§ 54. M. Huot also says, that granite is styled by mineralogists, a rock composed of lamellar feld-spar, quartz and mica, almost equally disseminated. If the mixture is equal, common granite is found.— Whenthe granite contains crystals of feld-spar of a regular form, and larger than those of the other constituents, it takes the name of porphyroïde granite, because, at first sight, it bears the aspect of porphyry.

It would be very interesting to follow the thought suggested by Buffon for the study of granite, and to avail ourselves of the reasoning of M. Huot; but this would take us too much from our subject, and we should occupy ourselves here less with the means used by nature in the composition of these Marbles and granites, than with those which may enable man. to avail himself of a part of them.

Nowhere, says Bexon, quoted by Buffon, can one conceive a more magnificent idea of masses of granite, than in the mountains of the Vosges. In a thousand places they offer blocks much larger than those we admire in the most superb monuments, and the broad summits and steep sides of these mountains are nothing but piles and groups of huge granite rocks, heaped upon each other.

§ 55.   Since the epoch in which these naturalists wrote, many surveys have been made, and we can say with them, that the Vosges contain the greatest wealth of this kind ; that they produce very fine granites of various grains and colors, several species of porphyry and richly colored jaspers.

The use of granite in the arts would be highly valuable for many purposes, particularly for water ducts, troughs, basements of manufactories, pedestals of funeral monuments, pavements or curbstones, props, supporting columns, and even for articles requiring polish ; for the most of the Vosgean granites take polish as well as marble, and retain it for a long time.

The principal objection is the difficulty of working them.   There is the certainty, at least, that neither frost, or water, or the sun or moon, which acts so powerfully on stone, can destroy the article which the hand of the artist has formed.   There is also the certainty that troughs, fountains, and vessels for holding water, will not leak, and that the necessity will be obviated, of cementing pieces, which is often done in blocks of·our best stone.

§ 56.   Marble workers use granite but little, on account of its hardness.   This is not their fault, but that of persons who do not take this difficulty of labor into consideration.   A little reflection will convince one that the transportation and setting being of the same price, it is more advantageous. to build works that will endure forever, without the trouble of repairing and renewing, than those that last but a brief time.

We will not speak farther upon the uses of granite as much that we would sav on this head would be a repetition of what we have already said respecting Marble.

Second Part.

THE ART OF MARBLE WORKING IN GENERAL.

SECTION FIRST.

CUTTING, WORKING, AND POLISHING MARBLE.

§ 57. The Art of the Marble worker consists in cutting, working, and polishing Marbles for the sculpture of chimney-pieces, facings, columns, pedestals, vases, basins, spandrels, rose-work, urns and monuments.

Marble workers are also commissioned with Marble pavements for compartments, stairways, vestibules, dining-rooms, baths, temples, chapels, and churches. A principal branch of their art is the sculpture of tombs and monuments; and in connection with this, they are required to engrave inscriptions upon Marble or stone, sometimes in black or white, sometimes in gold or silver. We will speak hereafter on this point.

Marbles are generally cut up in the same direction in which they are quarried; this is called sawing with the grain. Sometimes, however, it is necessary to cut them in a contrary direction; this is to saw against the grain. This renders them more difficult to work. Some marbles can only be sawed in the direction in which they are cut up.

The Marble worker is often obliged to rough hew, boast with the puncheon, and work, without the help of the saw, casings, rounded consoles, columns, and other articles with curved contours; sometimes, too, but rarely, he re-works, with the chisel, badly executed sawings; he then squares each piece with the saw or chisel, to give it the required dimensions, and finally mounts the Marble upon its stone core, and sets up his work in its place, which is not the least delicate part of the process.

The working of mouldings in particular, demands much time and pains; the first operation is to saw the arris, then to boast with a notched chisel, making several successive groovings, on account of the contour and expansion, in which but very small pieces of the material are taken, for fear of splintering it; and finally finish with small common chisels, which should be sharp and well tempered.

Cylindrical pieces, such as round pedestals, columns, urns, vases, etc., are boasted with the chisel, and then, if portable, finished on a turning lathe, by placing them between the points of large puppets, and giving them a continued rotary motion by means of a wheel, which is moved by a man in ordinary workshops, and

by water or steam in large establishments. When it
is impossible to place the pieces in a lathe, they are
thickly grooved, boasted with the puncheon, and the
desired contours obtained by means of thick panels;
they are then worked with a small chisel, which removes the dust, and thus prepares the Marble for polishing.

§ 58. A complete polishing includes five distinct
operations, namely :

Grinding, which consists in smoothing the roughness left by the burin. This is done by rubbing the
Marble with a piece of moist sandstone; for mouldings, either wooden or iron mullars are used, crushed
and wet sandstone, or sand, more or less fine according to the degree of polish required, being thrown under them.

The second process is continued rubbing with pieces
of faience, without enamel, which have been baked but
once, also wet.

If a brilliant polish is desired, Gothland stone instead of faience is used, and potter's clay or fuller's
earth, a sort of clay mixed with fine sand, is placed
beneath the mullar.

This operation is performed upon granites and porphyries with emery and a lead mullar, the upper part
of which is incrusted with the mixture until reduced
by friction to clay or an impalpable powder.

§ 59. Perfection of polish depends almost entirely on
the care bestowed upon these two operations, which

should be performed with a regular movement, requiring much patience.

When the Marble has received this first polish, the flaws, cavities, and soft spots are sought out, and filled with mastic of a suitable color. This mastic is usually composed of a mixture of yellow wax, resin, and Burgundy pitch, mixed with a little sulphur and plaster passed through a fine sieve, which gives it the consistency of a thick paste; to color this paste to a tone analogous to the ground, tints or natural cement of the material upon which it is placed, lamp black and rouge, with a little of the prevailing color of the material, are added. For green or red Marbles, this mastic is sometimes made of gum-lac, mixed with Spanish sealing-wax of the color of the Marble; it is applied hot with pincers, and these parts are polished with the rest. Sometimes crushed fragments of the Marble worked are introduced into this cement; but for fine Marbles, the same colors are employed which are used in painting, and which will produce the same tone as the ground; the gum-lac is added to give it body and brilliancy.

The third operation of polishing consists in rubbing it again with a hard pumice stone, under which water is constantly poured, unmixed with sand or other mordant.

§ 60. For the fourth process, which Marble workers call softening the ground, lead filings are mixed with the emery mud produced by the polishing of mirrors or the working of precious stones, and the Marble is rubbed with a compact linen cushion, well saturated with this mixture; the English rouge is also used for this first polish. For some outside works, and for hearths, paving tiles, etc., Marble workers confine themselves to this polish.

When the Marbles have holes or grains, as do certain Breccias, a lead mullar is substituted for this close linen cushion.

Finally, in order to give a perfect brilliancy to the polish, the gloss is applied. This is done by first washing well the prepared surfaces, and leaving them until perfectly dry; then take, again, a linen cushion, moistened only with water, and a little powder of calcined tin of the first quality. After rubbing with this for some time, take another cushion of dry rags, rub with it lightly, taking care to brush away any foreign substance which might crease the Marble, and a perfect polish will be obtained.

§ 61. It is necessary to observe that, in order to gain time and facilitate labor, many Marble workers mix alum in the water which they use. This mordant penetrates the pores of the Marble, and really gives it a speedier polish. This, however, is a fictitious polish, which spots very easily, and which is soon tarnished and destroyed by dampness. It is necessary, when purchasing mantels, tables, or other articles of polished marbles, to subject them to the test of water; if there is too much alum, the Marble absorbs

the liquid, and a whitish spot is left. When Marble
refuses this test, one may be sure that the polish has
been forced with alum, and, consequently, will not be
durable; it is very common on selling a piece of furniture of this Marble, to pronounce it a capital polish;
but this is a fraud to conceal that of the artisan.

Marble workers mount and fasten their works upon
plaster mixed with a third part of dust, as pure plaster repels the Marble, and causes it to swell out and
burst. These are joined together by cramps and gudgeons of iron and copper, which should be carefully
covered, in order that the oxides may not spot the
casings.

Mounting is an important point, for the Marble
worker as well as the proprietor. It is not uncommon
to see mantels broken by the force of the plaster, and
the angles and sharp arris of hearths are almost always broken off by the carelessness of the masons, who
trouble themselves less, as they incur but a trifling
responsibility.

Marble chimney-pieces are, or should be, lined with
lias stone or plaster: this is the same stone which is
generally used in bands for pavements.

ON THE MANNER OF WORKING MARBLE.

§ 62. The first care of the Marble worker should
be to procure those Marbles best suited by nature for
his work, whether purchased in the block, or, as is
most usual, in slabs of different thicknesses.

When in the workshop, he should examine each
piece, note its beauties, and endeavor to hide its defects, before even cutting or working it; this is a very
important point, both for his own interest and that
of the art. He should, when chance beauties are
found, endeavor, to cut them into two or three parts,
in order to multiply them; the height of the art consists in cutting them in such a manner, that these
happy accidents may be reproduced according to the
will of the artist. Thus, it is a piece of good fortune
to be able to cut a Marble for a mantel in such a
manner, that the collection of veins which form its
chief beauty, may be reproduced on both sides, and in
the middle of the mantel. But this rarely happens,
for the artisans cut the Marbles in the most economical manner, and this cutting throws these accidents in
the strangest positions.

This can be understood when we consider the calculations of most Marble workers. Thus, let us take
for example a block from which two console-tables are
to be made. There is a beautiful collection of veins
in the upper part; we saw it beveling, in order to divide the happy accident; it is reproduced, in truth,
but it is on one side on the top, and on the other the
bottom of the console.

The best way will be to have two such pieces, and
to cut them uniformly; but to do this, it is necessary
to be well served in the quarries, where the workmen
can see the exact contents of a block, from the one

which preceded its extraction and that which remains.

If the Marble worker chooses to order his Marbles ready cut, he must take such as are sent to him; and, instead of making his own choice in the quarry, he is never sure of obtaining the finest, and often chances to receive the most defective, for the simple reason that the finest blocks are often selected before they are cut.

Marble in slabs is almost always better sawed than that which is cut up in the workshops, because the tools of the large establishments are always better mounted, and better managed than those of the smaller ones; and I call all Marble yards small in comparison with the quarries, whatever may be their private importance.

§ 63. It is not uncommon to see works in Marble yards which were not executed there; they are sent there ready made, and even polished. It only remains to the artizans to double them, and to decorate them in the tastes of the purchasers; and they are often spared even this trouble by the furnishers, who employ themselves in the decoration as well as the execution of the most exquisite works. There is one great advantage in this; the wholesale furnishers have greater facilities, a more extensive choice, and less expense, and if a piece breaks from a defect or accident, it can be replaced by taking another from the block from which it was extracted; whereas, on the other hand, it would be necessary to order it at a great expense, and with an uncertainty of finding it, if the accident should happen in the Marble worker's shop.

Whatever may be the article which is placed on the bench, whether console, mantel, or tablet, all are worked in the same manner; with the mallet for rough-hewing, the chisel and burin for boasting and finish-ing, the sand-stone for planishing, and the pumice-stone and cushion for polishing.

§ 64. Besides the tools of which we have spoken, the Marble worker has in his shop pieces of sand-stone, hone, and pumice-stone, prepared in the best manner to glaze smooth surfaces, to round and groove mouldings, to destroy marks, stains and roughness, and to prepare a brilliant polish which will draw out all the beauties of the Marble, without concealing any of its defects.

When the piece is finished, and the flutings well grooved and uniform, the dust of baked clay, called *rabat*, of which we have spoken before, is used. This dust should be well sifted, and rubbed over the Mar-ble, either with a piece of sandstone prepared for that purpose, or with a coarse linen cushion, which should be moistened from time to time.

The workman sees the effect of his labor every mo-ment, when the marble is of a good quality; but when otherwise, he can only obtain an imperfect pol-ish; difficulties occur; soft parts drop off, mastics spring up, cracks become visible, and it is exceedingly vexatious when, after having lost much time, and wearied several men, the Marble worker is compelled to reject the stubborn and defective piece.

The more inferior the quality of the Marble, the longer and more difficult is the labor. When it is good, the artisan soon completes his task; he congratulates himself upon his work; but a little time is needed to finish the work so well begun; a few strokes of the *rabat* and of pumice-stone, and then the cushion, powdered with emery dust for the colored, and powder of tin for the white Marbles, or, which is still better, substitute, as we said before, a piece of lead, by which a finer and more durable polish will be obtained.

There are more expeditious methods which are employed in inferior workshops, but we shall say nothing of them, except that they are a discredit to the establishments which employ them.

SECTION SECOND.

OF SETTING UP.

§ 65. The setting up of chimney-pieces, patterns, plinths, etc., is at the charge of the Marble worker, as well as the plaster and other materials necessary to the consolidation of the work. This is the most delicate operation of his labor. There is little danger of mistakes when he does this work himself, but it is quite a different thing when left to the care of masons. Often, through carelessness, they set up a Marble without making sure that it will not warp, that it will not crack, that it is not above or beneath the flooring, that it does or does not rest squarely upon the wall, that the table beneath will be perfectly fastened to the mortar, the mantel or the band, in such a manner that it will not unhinge.

§ 66. This precaution is particularly necessary in setting up white marbles, which are apt to sag in the middle, when they bear only on their ends. This sagging of perhaps the half or one-third of an inch in the course of the year, is exceedingly disagreeable and ungraceful, the clocks being no longer upright, and the vases and candelabras inclining to the side of the curvature. A little attention, however, will prevent all these inconveniences.

There is yet another reason why the Marble worker should himself set up his mantels, his hearths, his moldings and patterns. For this work small claws are necessary to keep in place the different parts of the Marble. The mason often neglects these, and the action of fire or plaster causes a movement in the mantel or molding, which becomes so distorted as to shock the most unpracticed eye.

The same thing is true respecting the setting up of

plinths along the walls. This is considered of so much importance, that careful Marble workers always reserve this part of the labor to themselves, and in this they act wisely.

For all this work, plaster should not be used, lest the Marble might be warped or broken by its expansion.

§ 67. The reasons which we have just given, ought to be sufficient to convince Marble workers how much their own interest demands the setting up of works by themselves; but a more important one still remains; their responsibility. The proprietor, or builder, who employs a Marble worker, cares little as to what workman sets up the work, provided it is well done. When this is not the case, they are angry, and blame the Marble worker. They do not hesitate to accuse him of negligence, of incapacity, of deceit and unskillfulness; yet we see establishments decline, and fail even, against whom no serious charge has been made. The reason is obvious. As soon as the proprietor complains of the work, the Marble worker casts the blame upon the mason, and he in turn upon the Marble worker, whose Marbles he declares to have been warped and defective; and to settle the difficulty, he must appeal to the law. He prefers to be silent, to suffer the damage, but with the resolution of no longer employing one who had fulfilled his obligations so badly. This, perhaps, is somewhat rigorous, but it is the exercise of an incontestible right.

SECTION THIRD.

OF MOSAIC WORK.

§ 68. The modern workers in Mosaic use, at present, the black Marble of Farran, of Labal, the deep black of Argueil, of Pouilly, and of St. Cyr, in the suburbs of Lyon.

For blended tints, the ancient mosaists employed the Marbles of Florence, which are found near the Arno, and which, in general, are of an olive, dead-leaf color, umber and wood shades; they also used differently tinted flints, reddish violet, and brown.

It must be admitted that in lapidary paintings, above all, in portraits, nothing can better render the mellowness and transparency of reflex in the shade which oil paintings give us, particularly when the brilliancy is enhanced by the glow of the vitrified pastes. M. Belloni has profited by these resources so well in his Mosaic of the Car of Victory, that one must be forewarned, to know that it is a lapidary painting.

The Mosaics of the ancients are less fine and less finished than those of the moderns, but they are distinguished by a happy mixture of colors, a spirit and design which are wanting in the latter. They cut their Marbles in strips to form their cubes, and gave them the shape of dice. When prepared, they probably placed each color in a compartment, separately, as we now do.

The ancients, to collect their cubes, employed a mastic composed of lime, the dust of marble, and curdled milk or skimmed cheese, the sediment of which would form a line of the rich color given by the milk. M. Ritter, in his Collection of Swiss Antiquities, observes that the cement of the cubes of an Avenchon Mosaic is composed of a paste of pulverized yellow stone and linseed oil. To this, litharge may also be added.

When the mastic is very dry, rub it and polish it as usual, taking care to move the instrument or cushion evenly, so as not to injure the cubes, which are still soft, or the mastic, which has not yet acquired its full degree of solidity. The white Marbles, in particular, are softer than the others, and more apt to strike off.

After a little time, warm the Mosaic a little to free it from all moisture, and then finish by rubbing the whole with a cushion of cotton or soft wool, slightly moistened with linseed oil.

SECTION FOURTH.

ON THE VENEERING OF MARBLE.

VENEERING UPON WOOD AND STONE.

§ 69. The plating of silver, the veneering of costly woods upon common ones, and that of Marble upon walls, might have naturally suggested the idea of the veneering of Marble upon wood for pedestals of clocks, little articles of toilet furniture, or even for centre and all other ornamental tables.

M. Mudesse claims to have found a certain method of effecting this object, without the obstacle which the constant warping of the wood opposes to the preservation of the Marble, which is often broken by this expansion.

The purport of his ideas is as follows :

During several years, the use of Marble upon stone has greatly increased, despite the inconvenience of the enormous weight of the articles manufactured of the plated Marble, which has also caused their transportation to be very expensive.

Marble workers have sought to obviate these difficulties as much as possible, for ornamental clocks in particular, by hollowing out the interior. But this method, by leaving only a slight thickness of stone, compromises the solidity of the plated articles, and exposes them to many risks in transportation.

M. Mudesse has devoted much time to experiments in order to remove these obstacles, which have resulted in the discovery of a method by which veneering upon wood may be substituted for that on stone.

This new process, which is safe and solid in comparison with the old, offers every possible advantage to dealers in Marble.

The principal difficulty has been in veneering the

Marble firmly upon the wood without danger of its
breaking. The removal of this difficulty would procure the following advantages :

Firstly. The lightness of the plated articles, and
their consequent facility for transportation, with the
great reduction of price which would result in the diminution of the weight.

Secondly. The simplification of labor—as the wood
could be easily hollowed out as much as deemed proper without danger of its breaking, which often happens to the stone.

Thirdly. The absence of the oxydation of the pieces
of iron and steel composing the movement of a clock ;
an oxydation which is inevitably produced by the
dampness communicated to them by the stone, and
which, when dry, shells off and scatters its dust in the
pivots, which stops the working of the movement, and
proves an incessant cause of repairs.

" Thus," says M. Mudesse, " veneering upon wood
is preferable, in every respect, to that on stone."

M. Mudesse has also made many experiments in
the plating of Marble upon different metals, but has
found that none possessed the same advantages as
wood, in respect to resistance, solidity, and lightness.

The difficulty to be obviated was in the manner of
veneering the Marble upon the wood.

For this purpose, as Marble, particularly the black,
would break by heating it in the usual manner, M.
Mudesse places the slabs of Marble in a cauldron,

tightly closed, in which he lets them boil. He then takes them from the cauldron, and after this preliminary operation, he can, without risk, subject the Marble to the heat of the fire to receive a mastic of tar. The wood having been first prepared in a similar manner, he presses the Marble, coated with the mastic, upon the wood, and a perfect cohesion is effected.

The mixture of glue with tar, is found an improvement in effecting this veneering.

§ 70. We said above that M. Mudesse had unsuccessfully endeavored to plate Marble upon various metals : these possessing a smooth and polished surface, the substance which should fasten them to the Marble, could not incorporate itself with them intimately enough to join both and render them inseparable.

To resolve this problem, it was necessary to interpose between the metal and the Marble a third body, which should force them to perfectly adhere; this he effected by the use of sand paper

The cases of ornamental clocks are hollow, for the movement of the pendulum and other works. This hollowing cannot be effected on stone without detriment to its solidity.

But when wood is used, a frame is made of it, varying in form to suit the taste of the artisan, and the exterior parts upon which the Marble is to be veneered.

The following process is that which is employed in the plating of Marble upon zinc :

Take a plate of zinc of about the tenth part of an inch in thickness; make a frame of this of the form of one of the parts which compose the case of the clock, or whatever other article may be wished ; upon this form glue the sand paper, leaving the rough side outermost, and upon this rough side apply the Marble, having first prepared it by heating in a water bath, and placing between the Marble and the sand paper a coating of mastic of tar.

By this means, so perfect an adhesion between the Marble and the zinc is effected, that the Marble could be easier broken than removed.

The application of Marble upon zinc can also be effected by grooving the metal in every direction with strokes of the file, but this plating is imperfect : the sand paper produces the best results.

In case of need, coarse emery paper produces equally as good effects. The cohesion of the Marble upon the metal by the interposition of powdered glass or emery by means of glue, is not as perfect; the paper adheres better to the metal.

The inventor has given the preference to zinc over other metals, because it possesses both resistance and cheapness, and causes no other expense in the manufacture than that of cutting up to form the model.

Tin possesses neither the same resistance or the same cheapness ; sheet iron is dearer ; cast iron is too heavy; copper is expensive; while, by the application of Marble upon zinc, clocks or other articles can be manufactured and put in market at the same price as those veneered upon wood.

Taught by experience, M. Mudesse has joined to the processes of which we have spoken other means of execution, which we shall mention.

We have said that, in fastening the Marble to the metallic plating, the tar which is used in the application of Marble to stone will not be sufficient; for the metallic plate and the Marble do not possess sufficient roughness to absorb and connect themselves with the glue so closely, but that a slight shock will disjoin and separate them.

It was necessary, then, to find an intermediate mordant to effect the solid and inseparable adhesion of Marble to metals, and to replace the sand paper effectually.

When, in making the case of a clock for instance, it is desirable to apply Marble to a plate of zinc or any other metal, the parts must first be heated in a water bath, or over a furnace prepared for this purpose, and then, by means of a sieve, sprinkled with one of the following mordants:

Crushed glass, grains of emery of all sizes, copper filings, castings of any metal, finely rasped lead, any kind of powdered stone, such as sandstone, Marble, granite, pumice-stone, etc., even caoutchouc can be used.

When the sheet of metal and that of the Marble have thus received a sufficient mordant, they are joined with a coating of tar, which fastens together the roughness of these two substances, and forms a solid and inseparable whole.

The inventor, believing he had attained the highest degree of perfection in the application of his methods to the plating of Marble upon wood and metals, gives this abstract in a statement given to obtain a patent, in October, 1841.

" In the substitution of wood and every species of metal for stone, upon which, formerly, the plating of Marble was made, this problem has been resolved:

The production of perfect cohesion between two smooth surfaces.

This difficulty did not exist in the plating of Marble upon stone, because this being by nature grainy and spongy, it gave every facility to the clinging of the mastic, and the adhesion could be effected by the simple interposition of the mastic between the Marble and the stone.

But the same result could not be obtained between two smooth surfaces, as between Marble and metal."

"After numerous experiments to find a mastic, the grained composition of which might replace the roughness of the stone, I was convinced," says M. Mudesse, "that whatever might be the composition of this mastic, its sole interposition between the Marble and the metal could not produce an adhesion sufficient to resist the shocks and concussions attendant upon the transportation and working of these pieces.

I finally succeeded in discovering a process, which consists in establishing an artificial mordant upon the plates of zinc, or other metal, and that of the Marble, and then causing the adhesion of these two surfaces thus rendered grainy, by the interposition of common mastic, or tar."

The artificial mordant is fastened to the surfaces by means of paste, or other glue.

Any web of linen, hemp, or cotton, can also be interposed between the Marble and the metal; this web being covered with grainy substances, or artificial mordants, applied by means of glue.

These methods are not only applicable to the cases of clocks, but also to frame-works of every kind, and to all articles of ornament or luxury.

§ 71. It can be easily supposed that the above rules will apply to anything which is susceptible of being veneered with Marble, and M. Adin has used them for dressing-cases, work-boxes, and other articles.— The following statement was given by him on the twenty-second of March, 1842, of what he calls his invention:

" The Marble is first sawed to the desired thickness, and to the form required for the dressing-case or the work-box to which it is to be applied. When the pieces of Marble are thus sawed, the wood is prepared, (usually white wood, oak or fir) by cutting it in the same manner, but a very little smaller than the Marble which is to cover it. This wood is inter-lined with a shaving of beech wood, in order to pre-vent warping. This beech wood lining is only placed on the side which is to receive the plating of Marble; each piece of Marble is then applied to the corres-ponding piece of wood, and the adhesion is effected by means of glue or other mastic. When the Marble has thus been applied, the opposite side of the wood is thinly lined with rosewood or mahogany, in such a manner that this lining forms the inside of the box or dressing-case, which is thus prepared for receiving the necessary divisions and compartments. The four parts are then dove-tailed together, and the top and bottom parts fastened flatwise on the four sides with glue or mastic.

The box being thus finished, the outside is pumiced and polished, and any applications of gilding can be made.

The chief point of this invention consists in the idea, realized by me for the first time, of the applica-tion of Marble to the manufacture of dressing-cases, work-boxes, and articles of this nature, which have previously been made only of wood, cardboard, and leather."

There may be some little obscurity in this descrip-tion, but it will be perfectly understood by all read-ers who have any knowledge of the art, and they, probably, are the only ones whose attention will be attracted by it. This veneering is so much in use, and so valued, that we deem it unnecessary to enter into farther details respecting this new art, which is of so much importance, particularly in a commercial point of view.

SECTION FIFTH.

OF ORNAMENTAL MARBLE WORK.

OF THE SCULPTOR.

WHEN we speak of sculpture in connection with Marble working, it should be understood that this only has reference to the sculpture of ornaments, of which Marble is susceptible; the sculptor, in this sense, might be called an ornamentor.

This is a speciality, but it often happens that the Marble worker who performs these functions, takes the name of sculptor. We shall not speak at much length respecting the sculpture of Marble ornaments.

§ 72. What we have said has been rather to point out proper models to Marble workers and proprietors, by which to form and develop their tastes, than to impel them to devote themselves to sculpture. It is necessary to understand sculpture sufficiently to appreciate, if not to execute it. Medallions, capitals, friezes, flowers, rose work, acanthus leaves, the claws of griffins, lions, dragons, and heads of different animals, are nearly all which the ornamentor needs; and all these things are usually for chimney-pieces, or costly works which are purchased ready made, and are sculptured in the quarries, and are only ordered from the Marble yard to accord with some other ornament. This harmonizing depends as much on the Marble as upon the style of ornamenting.

The price of sculptured works depends on the talent of the artist, the delicacy and complication of the ornaments, the material of which they are made; for some Marbles are much more difficult to work than others; and, most especially, on their scarcity or abundance at the time of their execution. All these circumstances affect the price of sculpturing, and also the profits which the dealer can lawfully make. Another thing should also be taken into consideration, namely: the nature of the design given as a model.— An unusual design gives infinitely more trouble, and demands more time of the artist, than one which he is accustomed to execute.

There are also additional labors which should be taken into account, such as trials for the purpose of judging of the effect, transportation of parts of the work, the journeys of the workmen, the accidents which may happen, and the alterations which may be suggested by those giving the order. It often happens when the artist and purchaser have agreed upon a stipulated price, that they afterwards change the agreement which they had settled on.

On the other hand, if there is a chance of augmentation from the causes which we have just enumerated, there is also a risk of diminution, and even rejection, if the stipulated conditions are not precisely executed; and though men in a position to order great works would rarely wish to profit by such subterfuges, it is prudent to take every precaution to protect one's self from the chance of complaint.

There are also works which are so precious, by reason of the care and talent they demand, or by the name of the sculptor, that the same mantel, the same vase, or the same piece of marble executed by one artist, would have ten times the value of another, sculptured in the same style by an unknown or *mediocre* genius.

This difference in the value of ornaments applies also to the value of other works in Marble. It often happens that purchasers who cannot appreciate the difference, are astonished that of two mantels of the same Marble, one is worth ten and the other fifty dollars, or that of two vases of the same dimensions, one is valued at one hundred and fifty, while its equal apparently, is worth but fifteen dollars.

§ 73. In order to guard against deceiving one's self in valuations, whether in selling or in buying, it is necessary to take account of the labor, the material, and the perfection of the ornaments. It is impossible to indicate probable prices, since the price of to-day might be changed in a month or a year. Some usages of commerce authorize the merchant to reckon, in his valuation, the time which the article remains in his workshop, but this is a bad system. These are the chances of commerce to which we must submit, at the risk of the loss of confidence, and, perhaps, of credit.

SECTION SIXTH.

OF SCULPTURE BY ACIDS.

§ 74. There are secrets in every art, springing from the reflections of men of genius and often from chance, which render easy the execution of works which would necessitate an exceedingly tedious amount of manual labor, without the certainty of accomplishing its end ; such are the fillets, the chords, and the rows of glittering beads which are imprinted on metals with a simple mullar, the guilloches which almost form themselves by the perfection of the tools which are used, as well as the beautiful carving upon softened ivory and expanded shell, and the admirable designs upon paper hangings.

The sculpture of Marble without mallet, chisel, or burin, is still more wonderful, and not less easy of execution ; for this it is only necessary to know how to utilize acids.

Tables and chimney-pieces of white Marble are sometimes seen decorated with very delicate sculptures, which seem to require an immense labor, and for which it seems impossible that chisels or other ordinary instruments, however delicate, could have been used. The workmen, jealous of their secrets, concealed them in order to increase the price of their work, by causing it to be supposed that much time and pains were necessary to execute these beautiful masterpieces, whereas they were made with the greatest facility.

M. Dufay, having perceived that these works were too delicate to have been made with tools, soon discovered that they had recourse to acids, but experiments were necessary to specify them. Many acids caused the Marble to turn yellow, and were, therefore, inapplicable.

He also experimented upon several varnishes, until he discovered one which was easy to use, which dried readily, and was impenetrable to acids. Such is the course which one is always obliged to follow in the arts, in the simplest researches. The following is his process:

Prepare a varnish by simply pulverizing Spanish sealing-wax, and dissolving it in spirits of wine.

Trace on the white Marble, with a crayon, the design which is to be formed in relief, and cover this delicately with a brush dipped in the varnish; in less than two hours the varnish will be perfectly dry.—

Prepare a dissolvent formed of equal parts of spirits of wine, spirits of salt, (hydrochloric acid,) and distilled vinegar; pour this solution upon the Marble, and it will dissolve those parts which are not covered by the varnish. When the acid has ceased to ferment, and, consequently, will no longer dissolve the Marble, pour it on anew, which continue until the ground is sufficiently grooved.

It should be observed that, when there are delicate lines in the design which should not be grooved so deeply, they should at first be covered with varnish, to prevent the action of the acids upon them; then, when the reliefs have been made, the Marble should be well washed, and the varnish removed from these delicate lines with the point of a pin; then pour on new acid, which will groove it as deeply as desired—care being taken to remove it at the proper time.

It is necessary to observe that, when the acid has acted upon the Marble, it corrodes beneath the varnish, and enlarges the lines in proportion to its depth ; care should therefore be taken to draw the lines in relief a little larger than it is desirable to leave them.

When the work is completed, remove the varnish with spirits of wine, and, as the grounds will be very difficult to polish, they may be dotted with ordinary colors diluted with the varnish of gum lac. By coloring these grounds, or the reliefs which have been thus engraved, a beautiful effect will be produced, and one which, if the secret of this art should ever be lost, would cause them to be regarded in future ages as *chefs-d'œuvre.*

§ 75. M. Osmond, by a similar process, grooves not only Marble, but likewise copper and mother of pearl, and produces with facility effects which are seemingly difficult. For this purpose, he employs bitumen and acids.

The Marble being grooved, he also fills up the cavities in inlaid work with gold, silver, tin, sealing-wax, sulphur, crushed pearl shell reduced to powder, called *lithoïde*, etc.; every design executed in this manner, whatever may be its tenuity or delicacy, becomes indelible and indestructible by air or by the action of time. Any design can thus be engraved in three or four hours to whatever depth is desired, upon an article which could not have been thus decorated in a month's time by the chisel.

These designs can be made either in molding or in relief, without changing or injuring the Marble; every sort of writing, however delicate it may be, can also be thus traced; and the execution is very rapid, whether in groovings inlaid with gold or silver, or in relief which can also be gilded or silvered. It is by these processes that Marble workers execute a large portion of their work in the decoration of monuments with ornaments; and nothing is more beautiful, or more analogous to the destination of a tomb, than these lapidary incrustations which Time cannot destroy or even impair, until after repeated whettings of his scythe.

Do you wish to inlay with leaves of mother of pearl ? You no longer have need of the chisel to cut them; you make the grooves upon the Marble, and, with the aid of the needle, in a few minutes they are cut and the designs executed, of whatever nature they may be.

We might here repeat all that we said at the close of the article upon the veneering of Marble. There is some analogy between these two processes, both of which tend to increase the use of Marble to a great extent.

Without wishing to deprive any of the modern inventors of their deserts, we will conclude by quoting from a very interesting article found in the *Dictionnaire Encyclopedique*, published in 1785. In volume fourth, page 404, the following paragraph may be found :

" Some have succeeded in sculpturing Marble in very delicate designs by the aid of an acidulous liquor, which is formed by a mixture of spirits of salts and of distilled vinegar. Before the corrosion of the acids, the parts to be preserved in relief are covered with a varnish of gum lac dissolved in spirits of wine, or simply of Spanish sealing-wax dissolved in the same acid. The acid does not affect the varnish."

It would be difficult to say more in fewer words.— What do inventors deserve, when proofs are thus

placed before their eyes that all their pretended discoveries, with the exception of natural philosophy and
chemistry, which have made great progress, are but
reproductions of what was formerly practiced? In architecture, in joining, in locksmithry, in Marble
working, in painting, in sculpture, in gilding, there is
nothing valuable known to us, but what was used by
the ancients, and even in the *Renaissance.* If we
have, in respect to sciences, the right to call ourselves
glorious, in relation to the arts, it is our duty to be
modest.

Third Part.

OF OPERATIONS TENDING TO FACILI-
TATE LABOR.

SECTION FIRST.

MACHINES FOR THE RAISING AND REMOVAL OF BLOCKS.

IF the workmen are to be believed, the old machines which they are in the habit of using, are, and will continue to be, those best adapted to their wants. But as generations pass away, new ideas take root, and, ere long, the demand will be as great for new machines as it now is for the old ones. There are some, however, that are so good that it would be difficult to replace them with better; among these are the screw-jacks, the cranes for raising, and the carts, hand and wheel-barrows for transportation.

§ 76. Among the first rank in the raising of blocks we find the windlass, and its improvement, the crane, which are much used in the Marble quarries, but rarely for manufactured articles, unless needed to raise them, as in case of monuments or accessories to buildings. They are seldom used in the Marble yards where they would occupy much room; we shall therefore give but a brief notice of them; indeed a detailed description would · be unnecessary, as the windlass and crane are familiar to every one.

§ 77. It is well known that the windlass is composed of a cylindrical shaft, of a diameter proportionate to the use for which it is intended, which moves upon its axle by the aid of gudgeons inserted into fixed rests, sometimes in the form of an elongated X, and sometimes mounted upon an inverted T, and wedged upon a sleeper of squared wood or upon strong joists. Some windlasses are moved by cranks, some by wheels, and others by levers.

This may be called the primitive windlass. A cord or chain rolls upon it, and is firmly fixed in the shaft of the windlass, a hook being fastened to the other end, which is attached to the object to be raised.

This has been improved upon, and made more portable and solid, by the substitution of iron or brass for wood, and of gear instead of levers.

For the movement of the windlass, different mechanical apparatus is used, which is usually terminated by a wooden crank having an iron socket which crosses the wooden handle, to which it is fastened by a screw nut. This mechanism is more or less complicated, according to the weight which is to be raised, and the height to which it is necessary to raise it. The simplest apparatus consists of a wheel of a much greater diameter than the cylinder, mounted upon the same axle to which the force acting upon the circumference is directly applied. In this case, the conditions of equilibrium are those of a lever of which the arm of force would be the radius of the large wheel, and the arm of resistance the radius of the cylindrical shaft. The advantage of the power over the resistance can be augmented, by employing a set of windlasses joined together by cords passing around the wheel of one and the cylinder of the other. But instead of employing cords, another method is often used, which makes no change in the conditions of equilibrium between the power and the resistance; namely, notched wheels which work into pinions representing the cylinders.

The axles of these machines may either be parallel to each other, or alternately parallel and perpendicular, following the position of the teeth of the wheels; this method will considerably augment the force of the man, and will prevent many accidents; these, indeed, are almost always occasioned by the unskillfulness of one of the workmen employed.; the more the number is limited, the nearer is the approach to unity, and the less are the chances of misunderstanding. and consequently, of the accidents which are the frequent results of it.

THE CRANE.

§ 78. This machine is constructed by the union of several simple ones; the lever, the cord, the pulley

and the windlass. The principal piece is a lever of
from fifteen to twenty feet, according to the use for
which it is intended. It is suspended near the middle
on an axle or a vertical shaft, which revolves in a circular movement about the point of support. At one
end is a pulley or a cable, to which is attached the article to be moved. The same cable is then carried
back to the other extremity of the lever, and is communicated to the windlass by which the machine is
worked. The weight is not only raised at the pleasure of the workman, but he can also change its position from one place to another, by the movement of
the vertical shaft, around which the machinery revolves.

The crane is one of the most ancient vehicles
known; it is often improved upon by modifications of
the windlass, which is moved sometimes by bars, sometimes by gear, sometimes by horses, and sometimes
by steam, according to the demands of the manufactories or quarries by which it is used to ensure the
facility of removal of the manufactured articles.—
There are many weights which can only be raised by
the aid of cranes; its principal use is in extracting,
lifting, loading and exporting the blocks of Marble.

THE CRAB.

§ 79 This is more in use among carpenters and masons than among Marble workers, but it is often
employed in the quarries, and we shall therefore
speak briefly of it.

There are two species; the simple crab is composed of a triangle formed by joining pieces of wood, on the top of which a pulley is placed. The two sides, or arms, are crossed by the axle of a windlass at a certain distance from the base of the triangle, or ground. When a weight is to be raised, the crab is placed in an inclined position, and fastened with ropes attached to the points of resistance. The rope by which the weight is to be raised, is then passed into the groove of the pulley, and rolls itself around the windlass in proportion as the load is raised.

The double crab, which is employed in the lifting of heavy masses, is simply the union of two such sets as those of which we have just spoken. The crabs are propped against each other like the two uprights of a double ladder, when they are of equal force and height. In some cases it is more advantageous to have one shorter than the other; they are then joined at the top of the shortest in such a manner that the longest one projecting above, has the effect and supplies the want of the crane. In either case, the power of this machine is in direct proportion with the number of arms which are used and the length of the lever, or the size of the notched wheels and the radius of the windlass.

In heavy works of architecture, or of extraction of stone and Marble, the crab is often replaced by four similar posts, forming a perfect square, and running up to the top of the building. This frame is termi-

nated by two joists, or two stop planks, between which
a pulley turns, upon which a cord or chain continually
mounts and descends, by means of a windlass placed
upon the ground.   This frame work has several props
upon which men can be placed to guide the movement
of the weight.   By this means huge masses can be
raised and placed as may be wished, almost without
effort.

THE WINCH.

§ 80. The winch is simply a vertical windlass, having a shaft or a conical cylinder, around which a rope
or cable rolls, to which the weight is attached which
is to be moved to the desired point. It is not used
in the workshops, but is an excellent means of approaching the blocks worked, thus avoiding blows
and wounds which are often given by the ordinary
levers which are used in placing the polished pieces
on rollers, or those to be polished in place, after being
worked in the yard.

The vertical cylinder is surmounted by a head
pierced with holes, in which bars are placed which
cross it, and serve to put it in motion by the force of
the arm.

The winch varies in form and power, according to
the use for which it is designed. There are small
ones which, imbedded in the wall of the workshop, in
the face of the boards, greatly facilitate the fixing in
place of large sized articles.

They may also be used to bind together pieces which are to be joined with mastic, and to keep them in place in such a manner that they may be easily worked, and the welding consolidated. They may also serve as parallel vices, by means of two joists, placed horizontally or vertically, as may be wished. For this it is only necessary to lay down one of the stationary joists. They should both have holes in the two extremities, in which a strong cord is passed.

One of the end pieces, in which is a ring, is drawn behind the movable joist by the aid of a pin which is passed in the eye of the cord; the other end is fastened to the hook of the windlass. When the cylinder is put in motion, the movable joist approaches the stationary one, and draws towards it the article, the pieces of which are to be pressed. This is a much better method than that of loading the welded pieces with weights to secure their cohesion, and possesses the great advantage of neither breaking or scaling them.

We will suppose that a Marble worker wishes to make a vase of a large size; it is to be composed of four, eight, or ten pieces, more or less, which are to be joined by the aid of cement, or mastic, incapable of sustaining the weight of each of these pieces; it is evident that the use of the winch, by drawing to itself the two cords which surround the pieces of Marble, will permit him to work them in place, internally as well as externally, and to hoop them with iron with great precision, if this seems necessary.

THE TACKLE.

§ 81. This machine, which is of prodigious force, but extreme simplicity, is sometimes used in the shops of Marble workers to raise or bring forward pieces of great weight. For this, it must be fixed to a solid post by a ring proportioned to the force of the hook of the tackle, which is usually composed of three or four pulleys in brass or copper, revolving upon the same axle. A movable tackle is usually joined to a stationary one, in such a manner that the same cord may pass in the grooves of all the pulleys. The power should equal the resistance. We find in market tackles, such as weighing machines or steelyards, which are capable of raising six, ten, or twenty thousand pounds.

They are often made to bear up still more. We sometimes hear inexperienced workmen boast of raising blocks of twenty thousand pounds weight with a tackle of twelve; but these are often the victims of accidents which they might have shunned, by not imposing upon their machinery a service for which it was not constructed.

The tackle, when joined with the windlass or winch, will be of the greatest utility in large establishments, as it unites force to precision of movement. Stationed near a machine for finishing large blocks, it greatly facilitates the moving of them to try whether they are properly placed; it is also the means of sparing the strength of the workmen, and guarding them from many accidents.

THE JACK SCREW.

§ 82. The screw is an instrument which is well known in respect to its use, but which is often abused by not proportioning its force to the weight that is to be raised.

Why are they constructed of different sizes? Precisely in order that the workmen may suit them to the uses in which they are to be employed. If they made better calculations as to the weight of the loads, less of these instruments would be broken.

There are several kinds of screws. The simple screw jack is formed of a cap or strong box of oak, hooped with iron, in which a notched wheel moves up and down. On the top of this box is a hole, from which the head of the screw proceeds, which is turned with a pinion notched with teeth, to raise the weight which it is required to displace.

This works admirably when the screw can be placed upon solid earth which will resist the pressure of the weight of the mass; when the ground yields to this pressure, it is necessary to guard against accidents, to place the screw upon a paving-stone, or a flat or square piece of wood, capable of sustaining the resistance of the screw and the weight that is rais'd.

It is an admitted principle, that the power of this

machine is to the resistance, as the radius of the pin
ion is to that of the crank.   The screw is furnished
with two important agents : one is a kind of iron shoul-
der in the form of a strong claw, by which the load is
taken almost from the earth and elevated to a certain
height; the other is a catch which a bolt fixes after
the screw, in order to stop the notched shaft in which
it is placed when the weight is elevated to the point
at which it rests, which is according to the height of
the screw.   This catch allows the workman to rest,
and gives his assistant time to wedge up either the
screw or the mass.   When the mass is wedged, it can
be easily taken up again, either with the aid of the
claw or the head of the screw.

The second species of screw has several toothed
wheels furnished with pinions, with the view of augmenting the power of the screw; this is called a compound screw.

The third is the common screw, for firmly fastening
trunks, bales, or packets for transportation.

There is still another kind called nut screw, which
is employed for the same, or analogous uses.

It is very important, that whoever may use it should
not employ it in works exceeding its power, for when
its teeth are once broken, bent, or warped, it is repaired with difficulty, and never possesses its original
strength.

SECTION SECOND.

NEW MACHINE FOR RAISING MARBLES.

§ 83. In reviewing all the machines intended for raising and removing heavy weights, the most useful and most portable are found to be the screw, the crane, and the tackle.

The screw is more portable than the crane, but is ineffectual in raising heavy blocks; it can only separate them from the ground. The crane, on the contrary, can elevate them to any given height—this depending on the length and force of the rope, chain, or leather strap which rolls upon the windlass or wheel placed at the bottom of the crane, and the number of men who, being furnished with bars, put the machine in action.

The tackle serves the same purpose as the crane, but with more facility and less workmen; this can be adapted to a crane, thus augmenting its force.

An inconvenience of the screw is, its sinking into the ground if it is moist or sandy. A machine would be desirable in which these three might be united.—Such a one M. David How claims to have invented, the advantages of which he thus sums up :

Firstly. This machine is simple and portable.

Secondly. It not only moves the weight, but raises it above the ground.

Thirdly. It so well supplies the power of men, as to cause the strength of four to be more powerful than that of a hundred.

Of this machine, M. How gives the following description :

It is composed of three pieces of wood fifteen feet long, pierced in the top with holes in which a strong iron bar is passed, to which a tackle is hooked. The stake of the hinder one is immovable, and is carefully fixed in the ground ; those of the front should have free play ; they must also be spread apart, and fixed, in the ground.

When the machine is placed, a rope is passed around the wheels of the tackle. A pin of two inches in length—the upper part of which is flat and the lower part cylindrical—bears a ring in which the hook is inserted. This pin is about nine-tenths of an inch in diameter at its lower extremity, and grows somewhat larger towards the middle.

The end of the rope which passes over the pulleys, rolls over a windlass of some six feet or more. A workman then, with a chisel or burin, scoops out a round hole of a little more than an inch in depth, and as nearly perpendicular as possible, in the object to be raised ; this hole should be somewhat smaller than the pin, so that it can only be inserted by driving in with a mallet. When the pin is thus forced into the stone, the hook of the tackle is passed in its ring, and the ropes extended by means of the crank of the windlass ;

all that remains to be done is to place the persons necessary to work it, and, strange as it may seem, the heaviest mass, although only grasped by the pin, can be torn from its bed despite all the obstacles which may oppose it, and raised in such a manner as to be suspended in the air.

To explain this extraordinary fact, those who have had experience think that the pin does not penetrate the stone in the precise direction of the acting force, and that the mass is raised and suspended in the direction pointed by the pins. M. How is not of this opinion; he is confident that it is to the elasticity of the stone, not the direction of the power, that the effects produced are attributable. The pin, being driven by blows of the mallet into the orifice in which it should rest, is retained there by the elastic power of the stone, in the same manner that a similar pin would be fastened in a block of wood if driven in it by the same means; yet with this difference, that the power exercised by the stone upon the iron, is incomparably greater than that exercised by the wood upon it. This explanation has been confirmed by experience, as it has been found: First, that the force which lifts the mass, acts exactly in the axle of the orifice in which the pin is forced; secondly, that when this mass is raised from the ground, it can be made to take every position without detaching itself from the pin; thirdly, that while no effort can draw out the pin, one or two blows of the mallet will detach it with the greatest facility.

The force which retains the iron, varies in proportion to the greater or lesser elasticity of the stone; this force will be less in soft stones than in Marble, granite, porphyry, etc., and it is the opinion of the author that the trial can only be successfully made upon these last.

We can also say that, although one can conceive that to a certain point, and in certain cases, large masses of stone can be suspended in the manner we have indicated, it is much more difficult to explain how these masses can be raised in a multitude of inclined and horizontal positions, and how, admitting that it is to the direction in which the pin is enforced that its adherence to the stone is attributable; it is found that, while a constant effort applied in every direction to the stone does not detach it, a slight concussion produces this effect at once.

To prove this, the following experiment will suffice:

Take a pin of iron, force it into a block of granite in the manner which we have described, then, without arranging apparatus, try, by means of a cord attached to the pin, to draw it out in every direction, using the greatest possible force—all your efforts will be useless. This clearly proves that it is the elastic force of the stone, instead of the direction in which the cord is drawn, which retains the pin in its place.

It is even necessary, when apparatus is used, to pierce the stone perpendicularly, because, if pierced obliquely, there is reason to fear that the portion of stone between the iron and the surface will not yield.

It is surprising, in using this machine upon large masses of granite, to see how little hold is necessary to draw them from the ground; sometimes, when the pin is inserted but a third of an inch in the stone, it will be immovable, and capable of sustaining a weight of several thousands of pounds.

This machine, so simple that it can be put up in the quarries and fields as well as in Marble yards, deserves to be practically used. It is necessary to fasten the uprights strongly, and to proportion their strength to the weight to be raised; because if one of them should bend or become displaced, a shock would ensue which would stop the operation, and, probably, cause some accident.

SECTION THIRD.

TOOLS FOR ORNAMENTAL WORK.

§ 84. The carving-lathe and the wonderful results produced by it, almost, we might say, without the aid of the workman, has given rise to many ideas among

mechanics respecting machinery for flutings, moldings, mortises, and guilloches.

Machinery is seen in metallurgic establishments, in
which steel, moved by water or steam, cuts, polishes,
and grooves iron as regularly as a chisel; it is only
necessary for a workman to press a screw to cause the
tool to cut, while it removes at the same time the
chips from the article turned. It then planes down
and polishes flat surfaces of many feet in length, and
even grooves mortises of several feet, more easily and
more regularly than those of a few inches could be
executed by the hand.

It is time that stone and Marble take their turn ;
many happy attempts have been made, and a complete
success cannot be doubted as soon as the spirit of invention shall be turned in this direction.

This honor may be reserved for M. Beaumont of
Paris, who is earnestly endeavoring to solve this problem. He took a patent for fifteen years, in February,
1846, for the invention of a machine for carving stone.
His patent having not yet expired, no one has the
right to extract from it; but we can give the description which he has given of his machine in claiming his
patent. This is found in volume seventh, page 134,
of the collection of patents of invention published by
government.

Upon a strong table, by the aid of a cramp fixed
in the wall, M. Beaumont adjusts his machine, which
is ingenious, but difficult to be understood by those

who have not studied the designs. We will only say that it is composed of a drill-tool with a rotary movement, supported by an upper plate, dove-tailed, and pivoting, if necessary, to any inclination; of a lower plate with circular furrows receiving the groover, the pivoting drill-tool being able to take every inclination necessary for the execution of all figures; straight, convex, concave, irregular or ideal lines; (a bore in front for wavy moldings upon a flat surface, or another bore in the form of the shelf of a chimney-piece, intended for reliefs or hollows, can be substituted for this;) of a transverse screw at the end of which is a pulley and crank, used to draw the drill-tool to the right or left; of a pin fastened to the drill-groover, at the end of which is a handle for obtaining the pivoting necessary to the inclination of the bore; of a pulley with two grooves, which receives the leather strap of the moving power; of a grooved calibre-box fastened by a pressure screw in such a manner as to serve as the point of support to this singular machine, which follows every movement indicated by the moving power.

The exposition of M. Beaumont also contains many other details which we will not repeat, as they cannot be understood without plans and designs which we have no right to give, they being the property of the inventor.

MACHINERY FOR MOLDINGS OF MARBLE.

§ 85. Indépendently of machinery for sawing, boring, and fluting, machines are also used for straight or circular moldings. This is a method of labor-saving which deserves to be studied and perfected.

One of these machines, invented at Marseilles, has been described by its author. As we have never seen it, we will only give the exposition made in order to gain a patent of invention, which was taken on the eleventh of April, 1845.

This machine is composed of a brass tray, furnished with two, three, or four wings, which are also of brass, in the form of a swallow-tail. Each of these wings is formed by two bands of iron, spoke-shaped, which divide the circumference of the tray and depart from its centre. These two bands are joined at their extremity by a circular band resembling a felloe, and thus form the swallow-tail.

The tray, with its four wings, resembles a Maltese cross; the bottom of the tray, that of the bands which form the wings, and of the felloe, forming a

single, flat surface; it might be styled a tray with
two, three, or four branches.

The tray may be round, or any other shape which
may be desirable; (the length of the wings is suited
to the diameter of the largest moldings which are to
be made,) it is placed horizontally, and pierced in the
centre with a hole from which a vertical shaft proceeds,
which is fastened there, either with a bolt, pin, by
boring with a screw-tap in a contrary direction to the
rotary movement, or by any other means which may
be best suited to the work to be done.

The shaft is of an indefinite length; it is furnished
with a pulley by which the rotary movement is communicated to it; its upper extremity turns in a socket
in which a rope is fixed, which, returning by the pulley, is fastened to a balance weight, which it holds
suspended; it is principally by means of this balance
weight that the apparatus is made to weigh in its rotary movements.

The shaft is fastened by two iron wedges to two
frames fixed in the wall, or to two cross-pieces of oak
or iron, according to the locality, and the nature of
the work.

The bands forming the wings of the tray, are
pierced with holes at different distances from the centre. Plates of metal, bearing the impressions of the
moldings to be stamped, are then fixed to each of the
wings of the tray, by means of a bolt in each wing,
which crosses them, and which is fastened over the

bands forming the wing, by passing into two of the holes which have been made.

Each of these plates has two notches, in which are concealed the heads of bolts, which rest against the wing of the tray.

The holes which are for the stamped plates in which the bolts pass, should be as far from the centre which formed the said plate, as the corresponding hole, which is on the wing of the tray, is from the centre of the said plate; that is to say, that all the holes should have the same radius.

At the back of each of the engraved plates, two grooves are made, which divide the greatest circumference, and approach the centre of the swallow-tail; these are about the eighth of an inch in thickness, and pass down the broad side of the plate, as may be seen upon its back surface.

These grooves are in the place where the bands pass which form the wings of the tray; they are made to receive a hand saw with two claws which are firmly fixed in them, whilst the bolts which fasten the stamped plate are clasped upon the tray. Two hand saws can be attached to each plate instead of one, if desirable.

If it is necessary to strengthen the wings of the tray, instead of cross pieces a third band may be added, which must also be on a plane with the bottom of the tray.

All being thus adjusted, a rotatory movement is

given to the apparatus, by means of a leather strap which is passed over a pulley; for this, gear may be substituted.

The apparatus being thus put in motion upon the surface of the Marble, sand and water is passed between the wings of the tray; and in the rotatory movement, the hand-saw cuts the Marble circularly; after which, the weight of the tray and that of the apparatus being heavier than the balance weight, the tray descends, and the stamped plates pass over the Marble and retrace the moldings upon it.

When a round slab is to be partially molded, the inside of the stamped plate should be slightly inclined towards the centre of the tray; if the slab is to be fully molded, the surface has only to be left parallel with the bottom of the tray, placing a cross on it formed by two bands passing from one stamped plate to the other. The edges of the stamped plates are cut sloping or somewhat rounded, that they may more easily draw the sand with them instead of repelling it; this is also true of the cross.

If a circular form is required—that is, that the middle of the round slab should be entirely removed—it is only necessary to attach hand-saws to the interior circumference of the stamped plates like those on the exterior circumference, only observing that the handles of these saws should be attached to the convex instead of the concave part.

Instead of the holes in the branches which form the

wings of the tray, these same branches can be cleft longitudinally to the centre, so that the bolts of the plates of all sizes can fasten themselves upon the bands of the wings of the tray; but this does not seem as good a method as that of the holes.

Instead of hand-saws, an iron hoop may be used, which, passing round the edges of the stamped plates, should be fastened by notches or other means to the iron bands which form the wings of the cross.

SECTION FIFTH.

MACHINERY FOR SAWING AND MOLDING MARBLES.

§ 86. An Englishman by the name of Tulloch took out a patent of invention in 1826 for a machine for sawing stone and Marble, and which was also suited to the execution of moldings. The following description is given of it:

The principles of this invention consist—

First. That the movable frames which hold the saws or molding tools employed for sawing or cutting different moldings in Marble or in any other kind of stone, descend in proportion as the saws or tools move, in such a manner that these frames will have a constant movement which will advance or retreat in a horizontal direction, and parallel, or nearly so, with the blocks of the saws or tools, and that, furthermore, if the block of Marble or stone is softer on one side than the other, the sawing or molding resulting from the action of the saws or tools, will not advance more rapidly on the softer than on the harder side.

Secondly. That during the operation of sawing, the end of the saw frames rise a little near the end of each alternate movement in which they advance or recede, in such a manner that, at the end of each movement, all the saws fixed in the frames are alternately slightly raised to permit the sand and water which are usually employed in the sawing of Marble, to pass freely between the grooving of the stone and the cutting pressure of the saw : this is impossible if the saws are not mounted to rise in this manner.

§ 87. Another French mechanician has proposed the following method of sawing stone and Marble, which he thus describes:

" I first place the Marbles and stones which are to be sawed, upon the same plane, in such a manner that every stroke of the saw may move in the same line.

" I use common saws, the handles of which are united and joined together in such a manner that the set may form a single, many-bladed saw.

" My large pulley, vertically placed, and furnished with a crank, draws, with the aid of a movable bar, the set of saws, which is carried back to its point of departure by the bar, or by a weight suspended to a chain passing over the pulley, and attached to the last of the saws.

"To prevent the set of saws from turning aside at the commencement of the work, it will be necessary to guide it with the hand until the strokes of the saw may be formed.

"Thirty or forty saws can thus be moved with a small power, and two men will be enough to moisten them, and to set the machine in motion in case of its stoppage.

"*General Application.*—The natural effect of my double apparatus is, to give to a roller a rotatory movement in different directions; but as known mechanical means exist of converting one kind of a movement into another and different kind, it follows, therefore, that my machine is, in truth, a universal moving power, which can replace every known force in the different needs of arts. This substitution will be always advantageous, since the force of the new moving power is enormous, and its establishment less expensive than that of any other moving power of an equal force."

SECTION SIXTH.

MACHINERY FOR SCULPTURING OR REDUCING.

§ 88. Many artists have long been engaged in numerous experiments, with a view to the discovery of mechanical means of sculpturing, and of reducing or enlarging sculptured articles.

They have obtained successful results, at least for boasting, and for executing with facility certain works which, with the chisel, would have cost much time and pains.

M. Sauvage, of Paris, took out. on the third of May, 1836, a patent of invention for a machine designed to reduce or enlarge statues, busts, alto and basso-relievos, with all the figures comprised in basso-relievos. This machine is composed of blades of iron, copper and wood, which are arranged and divided according to the principles of the pantograph.

The machine is mounted upon a movable shaft, which procures for it three circular movements directed by a common centre.

Upon the right blade is mounted a quadrantal hoop adapted to a band, of which the lower end is fixed upon the extremity, bearing a tube which is intended to receive a metal or wooden rod, or a roller which is gently worked over the surfaces of the article to be reduced.

The extremity also supports a tube which admits burins, etching needles, or drills, for working upon any material, whether Marble, stone, wood or metal.

This apparatus is fixed upon a hollow rest, in order to be able to ascend, descend, advance or retreat, according to the proportions of the work to be executed.

Two vertical shafts rigged with notched wheels are placed in an iron casing; the upper extremities of these shafts bear slabs intended to place the original, and to receive the material for the reproduction of the copy.

These shafts turn in the same direction by means of an intermediate wheel, or by double leather straps.

§ 89. M. Dutel also proposed another machine in the same year, and has taken out several successive patents of invention and improvement.

" To demonstrate in the clearest and most precise manner, the plan of the machine of which I am the inventor," says he, " I have thought it best to give the designs separately, in respect to their different applications and uses.

These designs number four, representing four machines. The first is intended to reproduce, in any kind of material, sculptures in the kind called basso-relievo, and of dimensions equaling the model.

The second is designed to reproduce sculptures, as the first, of dimensions equaling the model, but of the kind called alto-relievo.

The third is suited to the reproduction of sculptures in the kind called basso-relievo, but of greater or lesser dimensions than the original model; that is, it reduces or enlarges it a third, one-half, or three-quarters.

The fourth is designed for and suited to, the reproduction of sculptures in the kind called alto-relievo, such as statues, busts, etc., but, like the preceding, of greater or lesser dimensions than the original model ; that is to say, it enlarges or reduces them one-third, one-half, or three-quarters."

M. Dutel, after giving a detailed description of his machinery, concludes with the following important observation :

" It is proper to say that the *fraises* of either of these machines can be replaced by tools of the same shape and size, but not cut out like the *fraises*, and not tempered ; so that they may be used with diamond dust, in case that hard stones are to be worked."

§ 90. A third Parisian, M. Duperrey, also took out in 1846, a patent of invention for fifteen years for a machine for sculpturing, which he improved upon sufficiently to take out a second patent on the twenty-eighth of May, 1847, in which the following observations are found :

" The original description, submitted with the claim for the patent, demonstrated that, by the aid of this new machine, one could obtain at pleasure sculptures in basso or alto-relievos, or even in guilloches, similar to those produced by the carving lathe. This machine permits the sculpture of several pieces at the same time, either exactly copying the model or enlarging it ; the proportions of course, being regulated in order to obtain the relative proportions of the different parts of the articles which are to be reproduced.

The original machine worked very well, but it did not produce enough articles at one time, which increased the cost of the copying too much. Furthermore, I have perfected several details which permit me to modify the construction of the whole, with the view of causing the tools to work during the going in and out of the sliding puncheon.

In the first machine, all the tools could only reproduce the same model, since they were all guided by a single key.

In the new machine the improvement is, that each tool can work upon one piece and reproduce a specific model, which can also be done by all the tools of the machine; still more, all the tools can work at the execution of the same piece, and all can be directed, by a single key, to work upon one model.

This new arrangement permits the manufacture, either of a great number of pieces at the same time after different models, or of a piece of large size in a very short time; as all the tools which the machine possesses can assist in the execution of the piece."

We will briefly add that this machine is composed—

Firstly. Of two parallel slides, placed horizontally —one being designed to support the model to be copied, and the other, the material necessary for its reproduction.

Secondly. Of a support in which the keys and the tools move; this support is placed between the two slides, and the upper part is rigged with keys which receive all the movements of relief of the models placed above these keys, in order to communicate them to the tools which are mounted on the lower part of this support.

M. Duperrey concludes his exposition and the description of his machine by this observation: Flutings for the feet of tables can also be made in the same manner, by placing the molding tools into the tool casings; then, by making a line under the key, flutings can also be made of the desired form, and in a number determined by the dividing plate which serves for the guillochage.

These accounts are of a nature to interest amateur artists greatly, but they exceed the practical ideas of the Marble workers; for which reason, we shall not extend our remarks upon this subject, to which we must, however, direct their attention.

SECTION SEVENTH.

OF MASTICS.

§ 91. Mastics for stopping up holes, leakages, or cracks in Marbles, must not be confounded with those which serve to cement them together, or to consolidate them perfectly; these are used for veneering or pavements. The first is made with gum lac, colored, as nearly as possible, to imitate the Marble upon which it is used. Sometimes the gum is mixed with Marble dust passed through a silken sieve; in other cases, little pieces are used, which are cut and adjusted in the hole or fissure to be repaired, and glued there with the gum mastic—the precaution being first taken to heat the Marble and the pieces, and to take measures for producing a perfect cohesion. The cementing mastics merit the attention of proprietors as well as workmen, because it is often on account of the use of those of inferior quality, that works in cemented pieces deteriorate and lose their value.

§ 92. In the first rank should be placed the thick mastic, composed of two parts wax, three of Burgundy pitch, and eight of resin; melt this, and then throw it into spring water to solidify the paste, then roll it into sticks, and, in using it, melt only such a portion as is needed for your work; this precaution will preserve its strength, as the remainder becomes more brittle by heating it anew.

§ 93. The Corbel mastic, which is used in the seams of the flagging of stairways and terraces, is easily compounded.

Take six parts of the cement of good Burgundy tile without any other mixture, pass it through a silken sieve, add one part of pure white lead, and as much litharge, steep the whole in three parts of linseed oil and one of lard oil, and preserve it in cakes or rolls as the preceding. All the materials used should be thoroughly dry, in order that they may perfectly mix with the oil which unites them.

§ 94. **Fountain mastic** is compounded of the rubbish of stone ware or of Burgundy tile, amalgamated with thick mastic in such a manner as to form a paste proportioned to the use for which it is required; this is one of the easiest to prepare.

Mastic of filings is employed in the same uses as the preceding, as well as in places which are usually damp, or which constantly receive water, as curb-stones, flaggings of kitchens, bath-rooms and water-closets, and stone troughs composed of several pieces, either separate or clasped. This mastic, which is very good when properly used, is composed of a mixture of twenty-six and a half pounds of iron filings, or of iron and copper, such as are found among spur makers, but which must not be rusty, four and a half pounds of salt, and four garlics; this is infused for twenty-four hours into three and a half pints of good vinegar and urine; it is then poured off, and the thick paste which is found at the bottom of the vessel is the mastic, which should be immediately used.

These mastics should be used upon materials which are perfectly dry, otherwise they do not incorporate well, roll up, and are repelled by the moisture. Therefore, in executing this kind of work, the precaution should be taken to choose dry weather, and to open the seams well with a curved, sharp instrument, finally polishing them with the chisel.

Before laying down the mastic, the dust must be removed from the seam by blowing into it with a common bellows; a long, straight, iron chafing dish, closed at the bottom, with the grate elevated about an inch to obtain a current of air, is then passed over the seam; this chafing dish is filled with burning charcoal, the caloric of which draws out the moisture from the stone or Marble.

The slightest dust or the least dampness, hinders the adherence of every mastic; water infiltrates, and, when it does not immediately affect it, it will glide through after the least frost, after which it is impossible to remedy it. It is these infiltrations which cause so many proprietors to object to flaggings and other works of this kind.

§ 95. The Dilh mastic is, undoubtedly, the best that is known, but its composition is yet a secret; it is very costly, and its uniform color of a dirty white, renders it unsuitable for many works in Marble, for which reasons it is not much used by Marble workers.

There are others which we do not strongly recommend, because we do not consider them sufficiently tested; we shall point them out, however, that they may be experimented on.

MASTIC FOR CEMENTING MARBLES.

§ 96. The Mastic used by Marble workers for gluing and consolidating Marbles is of gum lac, colored. But this mastic, which is applied hot, only produces a strong cohesion when the Marble is also heated, which it is not always easy to do.

No good cold mastic is known to Marble workers, and the discovery of one would render a very great service to their art.   The following recipe claims this merit

To compound this mastic, take—

Hydrochlorate of ammonia,	2 parts.
Flour of sulphur,	1 part.
Iron filings,	16 parts.

Reduce these substances to a powder, and preserve the mixture in closely stopped vessels.   When the cement is used, take twenty parts of very fine iron filings, add one part of the above powder, mix them together, adding sufficient water to form a manageable paste; this paste, which is used for cementing, solidifies in fifteen days or three weeks, in such a manner as to become as hard as iron.

MASONS' MASTIC FOR COATING THE INSIDE OF CISTERNS, BASINS, ETC.

§ 97.	Pulverized baked bricks,	2 parts.
	Quick lime,	2 parts.
	Wood ashes,	2 parts.

Mix these three substances thoroughly, and dilute them with olive oil.   This mastic hardens immediately in the air, and never cracks beneath the water.

SECTION EIGHTH.

UNIVERSAL CEMENT.

§ 98. To compound this, a quantity of mastic should be dissolved in highly rectified spirits of wine, only enough of the spirits being used to effect the solution of the mastic.

Then soak an equal quantity of isinglass or fish-glue until it is thoroughly softened. Dissolve this in a quantity of rum or brandy sufficient to form a strong glue, to which add half the weight of gum ammoniac finely pulverized.

Thus for thirty penny-weights of the mastic, thirty penny-weights of isinglass and fifteen of gum ammoniac will be necessary. The quantity of spirits and brandy depends on their quality; the stronger the liquors, the less of them is needed, and the better will be the mixture.

Warm these two mixtures together over a slow fire, and when they are well mixed, place them in bottles, which must be hermetically sealed. This cement becomes perfectly dry in twelve or fifteen hours.

When the mastic is to be used, the bottle should be heated in a water bath to liquefy it; the fragments should also be heated before sizing them, and the surfaces well cleansed, as a matter of course.

Those who give this recipe, say that glass, crockery, etc., when thus restored, are as solid as before having been broken, and that the seams are hardly visible; but experience proves that these seams, although imperceptible at the time of the operation, soon soil for want of the perfect polish of the remainder of the article; this diminishes the advantages of the cementing.

COMPOSITION OF THE ATELIER OF THE MARBLE WORKER.

§ 99. The *Atelier* of the Marble worker is thus composed :

Of one or several benches, stronger and lower than those used by joiners. This is very necessary, as articles of great weight are worked on these tables. (See fig. 33.)

Of several saws of different sizes. (fig 59, 60, and 63.)

The last is held by one or more screw nuts, one being placed as in fig. 60, the other in the middle.— The braces of this saw are often modified; they are formed here of a collar and screw nut; sometimes the flat bar is bored and rigged with teeth entering into these holes, to shorten or extend the frame. This makes a strong draught, which lasts much longer than a rope, and is not susceptible to the changes of the atmosphere.

Of sebillas, or wooden bowls for holding the sand and water which should be thrown under the saw. (fig. 61.)

Of wooden or metal ladles with long handles, to take from the sebillas the sand and water necessary for the sawers of the Marble, who can thus work the saw with one hand, moistening it with the other. (fig. 56.)

Of handsaws without teeth, used in cutting stone or Marble with the aid of sand and water. A skillful workman often confines himself to making a deep groove in the Marble or stone, and then by a quick blow, separates the two pieces. (fig. 62.)

Of martelines, a kind of iron mallets pointed at one end, and diamond shaped at the other, which serve to pierce and shell off the Marble without splintering it. (fig 34.)

Of marteline chisels, used for the same purposes, and worked with the aid of the sledge hammer or mallet. (figs. 2, 4, 19, 20, and 64.)

Of puncheons. (fig. 5.)

Of a square etching needle. (fig. 1.)

Of etching needles called *houguettes*, partly flattened, and sharp. (figs. 8, 9, 27 and 28.)

Of hooks for sinking and levelling cavities. (fig. 10.)

Of round nosed chisels, used for the same purpose. (fig 11.)

Of sharp edged and notched scrapers for sinking flutings. (fig. 12.)

Of scrapers for the same purpose. (fig. 19.)

Of parting tools; a kind of flattened files, bent round and steeled at each end, to smooth those places most difficult to penetrate. (fig. 31.)

Of parting tools in round file, and half flattened in rasps, used for the same object. (fig. 22.)

Of German files, flattened on one side, and partly rounded on the other. (fig. 16.)

Of round files. (fig. 14.)

Of rasps, partly rounded on one side, and flattened on the other. (fig. 13.)

Of rasps in round file. (fig. 23.)

Of gravers or burins. (fig. 27.)

Of clasps. (fig. 28.)

Of wimbles, upon which augurs are fixed for boring the marble. (fig. 36.)

Of mallets. (fig. 64.)

Of iron sledge hammers. (figs. 65 and 66.)

Of hinged compasses. (figs. 68 and 71.)

Of compasses of depth. (figs. 53 and 54.)

Of iron squares. (fig. 43.)

Of levels. (fig. 77.)

Of rules. (figs. 47, 48, and 49.)

Of shifting bevels, or hinged squares. (fig. 46.)

This nomenclature is not complete, but it contains all the essential tools.

We have not spoken of cushions, or chafing dishes, or of pots for melting mastic, because the form of these is immaterial.

The tools we have indicated are used by twos, threes, or sometimes by dozens, according to the nature of the work, and the number of workmen employed in the establishment. It is necessary to say, however, that the more one has, the more are lost, or even broken, because the workmen take much better care of the tools when they are few, than when they can easily conceal all traces of their carelessness. Notwithstanding, one should have a great number of the sharp and edged tools, else much time will be lost in going to the forge or grindstone.

There is a simple method of avoiding the abuses of which we have just spoken, and one that is in use in some Marble yards; namely, that of giving the works by the piece, without furnishing the tools.

Fourth Part.

OF ARTIFICIAL MARBLES AND STUCCOS.

SECTION FIRST.

OF THE IMITATION OF MARBLES IN GENERAL.

§ 100. ARTIFICIAL Marbles have one incontestable advantage over the natural ones; that of composing surfaces of a great extent without seams or clasps, and of adhering so closely to the mason work that, when dry, they form part of the same body. Of all the methods of imitating Marble, there is none better than the composition of stuccos which has been long in use; these produce a beautiful effect in buildings. We shall explain the manner of their composition and application. We shall then speak of other artificial Marbles, of painting upon and coloring Marble, and shall conclude this part with interesting information relative to the manufacture of Venetian terraces.

SECTION SECOND.

OF STUCCOS.

§ 101. Stucco is a composition of a mixture of slaked lime, chalk, and pulverized white Marble tempered in water, designed to imitate different Marbles used in the interior of buildings or monuments.

There are different species of it, which may also have different bases.

Lime was formerly considered the only base of stucco. Our ideas have become greatly modified in this respect, but it is not yet proved that that which we make is superior to that of former times.

However this may be, as the hardness which the plaster may acquire is the most essential point in this art, it is to this that the workmen should first apply themselves.

This wholly depends upon the degree of calcination which is given to the plaster; and, as the stone which produces it is susceptible of some slight difference in its intrinsic quality, according to the locality in which it was found, one must study the degree of calcination necessary to give the plaster the greatest possible degree of hardness. The ideas which we give here relate only to the plaster of Paris.

Break the plaster stones in pieces somewhat larger than a large nut, put these in an oven heated as if for baking bread, and close the mouth of the oven. After some time has elapsed open the oven and take out one or two of the pieces, break these with a hammer, and if the calcination has penetrated to the centre of the piece so that a few bright points can be seen there, it denotes that it has arrived at its point of perfection; then draw out all the plaster as quickly as possible with a rake. If many of these brilliants are seen in the breakage, or none at all are visible there, it proves in the first case, that the stone is not sufficiently calcined, and, in the latter, that it is too much so.

Although the plaster becomes very hard when properly calcined, the surface is filled with a multitude of pores, and the grains are too easily detached from it to admit the polishing of it as of Marble. To remedy this objection, the plaster is diluted with water in which glue has been dissolved, which, filling the pores and fastening the grains together, permits the leveling and removing of the half of each grain, thus forming the polish.

Flanders glue is commonly used; some, however, mix with it isinglass, and even gum Arabic. Hot glue water is used for the solution of the plaster, as the want of solidity of the plaster, especially when it is not supported, demands that a certain thickness should be given to the works; to lessen the expense, the body or core of the work is made of common plaster, which is covered with the composition of which we have just spoken, giving it about an inch in thickness.

When the work is sufficiently dry, it is polished in nearly the same manner as the veritable Marble. A kind of stone is commonly used which is quite difficult to procure. This is a species of *cos* or coticular stone, which has finer grains than the sandstone, and which are not so easily detached from it. Pumice stone may also be used.

The work is rubbed by the stone in one hand, the other holding a sponge filled with water, with which the spot which has just been rubbed, is instantly cleansed, in order to remove what had been left on the surface of the work; the sponge should be frequently washed and kept always filled with fresh water. It is then rubbed with a linen cushion, with water, and chalk or tripoli stone. Coals of willow, finely pulverized and sifted, or even pieces of whole coals are substituted for this to penetrate better to the bottom of the moldings, water being always used with the sponge which absorbs it.

The work is finished by rubbing it with a piece of felt soaked with oil and finely powdered with tripoli stone, and afterwards with the felt moistened with the oil alone.

When a color is wished in the ground, it is only necessary to dilute it in the glue water, before making use of it to temper the plaster.

The stones for polishing can be adjusted to pieces of wood after the manner of jointers, or other joiner's tools; the surfaces of the work can thus be better prepared and the moldings more exact; it must not, however, be forgotten to always wash it in proportion to the rubbing.

When any particular Marble is to be imitated, dilute with warm glue water, in different small pots, the colors which are found in the Marble; with each of these colors temper a little plaster, then make of each a pebble nearly as large as the hand, place these pebbles alternately one above another, making those of the prevailing color more numerous, or thicker.

Turn these pebbles, thus arranged, upon the side, and cut them in slices in this direction, instantly spreading them upon the core of the work, or upon a flat surface.

By this means, the fantastical design of the various colors with which the Marble is penetrated, will be represented. If it is desired to imitate the Breccian Marbles, mix in the composition of these pebbles, when spread upon the core, pieces of plaster of different sizes tempered with the color of the Breccia, and these pieces, being flattened down, represent it very well. It should be remarked that in all these operations the glue water should be warm, without which the plaster will set too quickly, without giving time to work.

§ 102. When objects are to be represented on a colored ground—such as forests, landscapes, rocks, and vases of fruit and flowers—design them upon paper. Then puncture the outlines of the designed figures, place them on the ground work when the polishing is nearly finished, and pounce them with a color differing from that of the ground ; that is, of a black or red if the ground is white, and of white if the ground is black. Preserve the outlines marked by the pounce by sinking them deeply with the point of a shoemaker's awl, after which, with several awls converted into small chisels by breaking off the points and sharpening them upon a grind-stone, remove all the ground which is included in the outlines of the ground which has been traced, thus forming cavities on the ground of about the third of an inch in depth.

§ 103. When all that is contained within the outlines has been thus removed, procure several little pots or cups holding sand from the fire or hot ashes, upon which pour glue water mixed with different colors; take a little of the plaster in the palm of the hand, color it more or less by carefully mixing it with the colored water, stir up the whole upon the palm of the hand with a painter's coloring knife, until the plaster begins to acquire some consistency, then take with the knife a quantity deemed sufficient, which place on one side of the interior of the cavity of the figure to be represented, pressing it with the knife, and smoothing the surface of the colored plaster which has just been placed, and which joins the outlines of the figure.

Then mix immediately in the hand another colored plaster, but of a lighter shade than the first, which place in the same cavity, by the side of the first; prepare four or five needles, by thrusting them parallelly by the head into a small stick like the teeth of a comb, with which mix the last color slightly with the first, so that the passage from one shade to the other may not be perceptible, and that the degradation may be visible.

Continue thus to place the brighter shades on the side of the light, until the excavation of the figure to be represented shall be wholly filled. Finally, flatten the whole lightly with the knife, and leave it to dry.

If, after the polishing, it is perceived that the shades are not distinct in any place, hatchings may be made in this place with an etching needle, and a darker colored and very liquid plaster inserted; these hatchings must be quite deep, that they may not be destroyed by the polishing which must afterwards be given to the whole work. This last method is used for cutting out the leaves of trees, plants, etc.

Undecided figures—as ruins, rocks, caverns, etc.— generally unite much better in this kind of painting than figures which demand exactness in the shading and correctness of design.

The paintings are polished in the same manner as

the grounds, and if any little holes are discovered while polishing, fill them with plaster thinly diluted with glue water, and of the same color. It is even common, before using the oil for the polish, to pass a general tint of colored plaster and very clear water over the whole surface, in order to stop these small holes.

For all these operations the best and finest plaster should be chosen; that which is transparent seems to merit the preference.

For the colors, says the author of this process, all are suitable which are employed in fresco painting.

As it may seem strange that, in this manner of painting, we should have directed the use of the palm of the hand as a palette, we will give the reason for it. When a person dilutes the plaster with the colored water, he is obliged to use a certain quantity of water which would run off if placed upon a palette; by making a hollow in the palm of his hand, he retains it, and, by extending his fingers in proportion to the setting of the plaster, this singular palette, which was at first hollow, becomes flat when necessary. In addition to this, the heat of the hand prevents the plaster from setting too quickly.

Stucco is used either for ornaments, or for facings upon coats of impression: these last are composed, according to the methods described by Vitruvius, of several layers of mortar made with lime and pozzolaira. The stucco which was called by the ancients *opus albarium*, on account of its whiteness, or *mar-moratum*, because it imitated Marble, which was also included in its composition, was placed upon the last layer of the coat; this is of a finer and thinner paste. It seems to have been made with a species of foliated gypsum, calcined and pulverized, which produced a beautiful plaster. When using it, the workmen mixed with it the same stone pulverized, but not calcined; in order, doubtless, to replace the Marble dust, they compressed this last coating to give it more consistency and lustre. Some visible traces of pressure which have been found in several places, perfectly accord with what Vitruvius has said, and have even given reason for the conjecture that the instrument used in this operation, called by him *baculi*, was a kind of metal rule, light enough for the ends to support the prepared bands which serve as regulators to the workman.

§ 104. Such were the methods of our ancestors, and in practicing them they made in stucco the panels, columns, and pilasters which excite the admiration of men to whom ornament in architecture is a pleasure, and a means of satisfying a noble pride—since it cultivates a taste for the beautiful, and encourages the development of the arts.

It has long been observed that the palaces, chateaux, and houses in which stucco was employed for peristyles, stairways, and banquet halls, were always embellished with paintings, columns, and vases, either in concurrence with the stucco, or in the neighboring apartments. We have never seen anything more beautiful than the chateau de Mereville, on the beautiful estate of that name, in which M. de la Borde has collected all the choicest productions of the arts.

This hall was adorned with columns of white stucco, between which were panels of the same style, in which was hung four beautiful marine pieces of Vernet.

One can easily imagine that, entering in such a room as the peristyle of the apartments, they would penetrate into saloons of the greatest magnificence.

The use which has just been made of stuccos in the Palace of Foreign Affairs, on the banks of the Seine, also supports what we have just said. Thus stuccos are not enemies of Marble; on the contrary, they increase the demand for it.

It is not advisable then to neglect them; we should, on the contrary, encourage all essays tending to diminish their price, and to render them popular.

We will speak, then, of processes indicated in 1836, by a Mr. Burrows, an Englishman, who imported among us methods of manufacturing stuccos and cements in hard stones.

" In the first place," says he, " for a plaster cement, I take a certain quantity of this material, which I reduce to a fine powder by the means ordinarily used for the manufacture of plaster of Paris; or else I take a certain quantity of casts of other articles which have been made of plaster of Paris, and reduce them to a fine dust by the action of fire, or by pulverizing them with a pestle.

" I then mix a solution of the following materials: Nine ounces of alkali (of the best American potash,) in six quarts of water; this solution should be neutralized with some acid, sulphuric acid is the best for this purpose. The solution must be stirred up, adding the acid gradually until the effervescence ceases; then add nine gallons and a half of water, making about eleven gallons of water in the whole. If any other alkali is employed, the quantity of water should be varied in proportion to its force; the water thus saturated, should be mixed with a sufficient quantity of the powder to acquire a consistency, or a condition suitable to be used or molded, whether in slabs, bricks. or in any other forms, which are then left to dry, and afterward subjected in reverbatories, ovens, brass crucibles of the kind used in gas works, or by some other means, to a sufficient degree of heat to bring them entirely to a red heat. If these articles are not heated entirely red, the parts which are not sufficiently calcined will be softer and less durable than the cement which has attained a proper degree of calcination.

" The quantity of the solution necessary for the mixture is about half of that of the prepared powder.

§ 105. " Secondly, for a limestone or chalk cement, I take a quantity of limestone or chalk, which I crush, and submit to the usual process for burning or calcining lime. If I use the last process, I then reduce the lime to powder, either by exposing it to air, or by diluting it with water in the ordinary manner, (the dissolution by air is the best,) and treat it with a solution of alkali and sulphuric acid, as has been described for the mortar of Paris.

"But as less water is necessary for the mixture, the solution should be proportionably stronger. I dissolve nine ounces of alkali, of the best quality, in six quarts of water, to neutralize with the sulphuric acid in the manner explained for the Paris cement. I then add six and a half gallons of water, or perhaps a trifle more, and manipulate the solution to form slabs, which, when dry, I calcine in the manner described for the plaster cement. The solution necessary for the mixture is about a third part of that of the prepared lime. If the powder of plaster, chalk, or lime is used without being calcined, the calcination should be made in regard to the force of the liquid, and in proportion to the smallest quantity necessary to that object. -

" The solution of alkali without the addition of the acid, can be employed for the composition of a cement of the powder of plaster, provided that it is afterwards calcined, but such a cement will not be as good as those made according to the methods which have been described.

" Cements of the powder of lime and chalk can also be made with a solution of acid; namely, two ounces, Troy weight, of sulphuric acid, dissolved in six gallons of water, and then calcined as before explained. But the cements made in this manner will not be as good as those made by the other methods indicated. The processes of incorporation and of calcination for these cements, and for the cement of plaster with alkali, are the same as those before explained."

After having described the methods or processes for the composition of hard cements by a mixture of alkali and sulphuric acid with the powder of plaster, chalk or lime, and their subsequent calcination, by means of which the desired results with their advantageous qualities are obtained, Mr. Burrows adds: I shall now proceed to explain the manner of using them, and, as the cements made of the powder of calcined plaster, and those made of the powder of lime, possess different qualities, it will be necessary to establish a distinction between them.

§ 106. " I shall first speak of the cement made with the powder of plaster.

" The bricks or slabs before described, having been first reduced to powder and passed through a sieve in the manner used for hard cements, should be mixed with sand or gravel, and as the cement should produce no sensible heat while solidifying, it is desirable that the sand employed in the mixture should proceed from mineral or vegetable substances; for this reason, well calcined or vitrified sands are the best for this use, and for any mortar or stucco that can be mixed or applied in the same manner as the cements of lime and other calcareous cements. As this plaster can be employed for coats of impression or other uses in which a slight absorption is desired, care should be taken not to put too much water in the mixture. It will generally be sufficient to put in a fifth or sixth part of the quantity of the materials. But it must be observed that, in this case, the success will still depend much upon the nature of those of which it is made. The same rule will serve for the application of cement without sand, whether employed alone, or as a light coating upon a stucco with sand.

"If a particular Marble is to be imitated, the paste should be applied to a very smooth surface. It is afterwards polished, and the colors can then be varied if they have not been amalgamated during the application."

§ 107. "I shall now describe the manner of using the cements made with the powder of lime and chalk.

"These cements, when fresh, produce much heat in solidifying. There is, therefore, less danger of their after deterioration when they are mixed with common sand, which should be vitrified, or calcined, as has been already said. The chalks having been pulverized, should be mixed with sand and employed in the same manner as the calcareous cements.

"From this, it is evident that the sands which have been described as being used in the application of my invention for stucco and other objects, can be mixed with the powdered plaster, lime, and chalk when the acids and alkalies are added, and that they are then subjected, with the other ingredients, to the action of heat or calcination, in which case it will not be necessary to add any sand when using them ; and also that other alkalies or acids than those before mentioned can be employed, although, as none which I have experimented upon have succeeded as well, I give them the preference."

PERFECTED CEMENTS.

§ 108. Madame Bex of Paris, not finding the processes of which we have just spoken sufficient, claims to have discovered a method of less limited application, and which can particularly be extended to guard against dampness.

In pavements, flagging, and application upon the walls of ground floors, she has obtained, she says, the most successful results. This cement, which is as hard and compact as Marble, thus possesses those qualities of impermeability termed waterproof.

Stucco, on the contrary, being porous by the nature of its composition, is therefore easily accessible to dampness, which not only destroys its lustre but is a rapid cause of its deterioration. On this account it has not been employed for pavements and other uses before mentioned.

In order to obviate these inconveniences, Madame Bex has sought to ally stucco, as well as all other analogous compositions, and even soft and porous stone, with bitumens and natural vegetable, mineral and other bituminous mastics; that is, to line, in some sort, the stucco with these bitumens in such a manner as to thus preserve it from all humidity.

"When pavement or flooring is to be made, it is commenced by pouring the bitumen in molds of various shapes and sizes; before it cools, fragments of bricks, tiles, stones of all kinds, and even of wood, iron, brass, copper, lead, zinc, or any other material, are thrown into it.

"Before placing the stucco upon the bitumen, what is technically called a *gopté* is made upon the materials which have been put in it; the stucco is then tempered upon a table, and glue water and the colors necessary to the Marble to be imitated, mixed in it.

"The stucco being thus compounded, a cake of it is made upon the table; this cake is cut into slices of four-fifths of an inch in thickness, more or less. These slices are forcibly pressed into the mold in such a manner as to unite with the substances incrusted in the bitumen as well as with the bitumen itself, after which the stucco is polished by passing sandstone over it with a *martin*, (a brass plate mounted upon stone.) The pores which are found in it are then stopped, and it is rubbed again with pumice to smooth it. Stones for polishing copper are used in the commencement of the polishing, then clear stones, and it is finally finished with touchstones.

"Floorings may be made of a single piece, in courses, or in squares as may be judged most proper.

"Applications of stuccos against walls are made by the same processes as those used for floorings or pavements.

"This useful application will give a considerable increase to the use of stucco."

§ 109. It is doubtful whether this process of Madame Bex will perfectly apply to the proper stucco. The omission of indicating the quantity and quality of bitumen and other ingredients which she employs, will probably somewhat hinder the use of it by workmen.

But the following recipe is simpler and easier, and is much used. Take the best plaster that can be procured, crush it, bake it as much as possible, crush, sift, and temper it in a solution of Flander's glue in water, let it dry, polish it with pumice and tripoli stone, and add a lustre with soapsuds and oil.

In the "Lime Burner's Manual," we have described several other processes for the composition of stuccos, analogous to those of which we have just spoken.

Among other processes for coloring stuccos and giving them the appearance of Marbles, baked clay and metallic oxydes are used. These are the most solid. Oxyd of lead, ochre scorched and calcined, red ochre, and Roman vitriol baked in an oven, are also used.

One can also employ the oxyde or carbonate of copper, powdered green enamel, drops of forges, powdered scales of iron, etc., etc. The artist who is to make the imitation, must calculate the effects of the mixtures and the quantities to mix in order to produce the colors which he wishes to obtain, without losing sight of the fact that these substances produce very different results by the action of heat.

No book can point out the means of giving to the polishing of stuccos what is called a *coup de main.* This must depend on the practice and the skill of the workman. The Marble worker who polishes well calcareous stones, will also polish stuccos well. The rules for success are the same in both operations.— Above all, it is important to do nothing roughly, and to always keep the work perfectly clean with a sponge dipped in clear water. The cushion which is used should contain tripoli and chalk finely sifted, and when the surface is perfectly smooth, the lustre is given by rubbing it lightly with a piece of grey felt, sprinkled with finely powdered tripoli, and then, in the last place, with another piece of felt moistened only with oil. We cannot recommend too much care that, when a polishing operation is to be performed, the piece to be polished should be perfectly freed from all the humidity contained in itself or acquired from the atmosphere.

§ 110. When the stucco was used among the ancients to form ornaments, it was worked, says Vitruvius, in two ways, either with the boasting tools, or in the mold. When they wished to make, we suppose, a bas relief or large ornaments, the workman designed upon the coat of impression, with the point of the boasting tool, the outlines of the figures which he wished to represent, and then modeled them of the paste of the stucco as our modelers do with clay.— The material dried too quickly in the hand of the workman to permit of any alterations. Thus a great facility of execution was necessary to succeed in this work, which fact renders the beautiful compositions of this kind found at Herculaneum and Pompeii still more worthy of admiration.

§ 111. The second method was employed for small successive works, such as ornaments for cornices, framings and ceilings. When the coat of impression was set in the necessary place, a mold was applied which left upon the fresh surface the desired imprint; the chipped edges were then adroitly raised, and the ornament remained simply and immovably fixed. The seams of the mold can be plainly observed in all parts; besides, it would be difficult to imagine that these different ornaments were first prepared, and that they applied them like the pieces of facings, or bas reliefs; the extreme tenuity of some of the details would render this impossible.

MOLDINGS IN STUCCO.

§ 112. When moldings are made in stucco, they can be jutted out with bores as in mason work, or if these

bores are small, they may be fitted to a wooden joint-
ing plane.   To give a polish to all the indented angular parts, instead of a cushion of linen or felt, a piece
of willow coal, or even of common coal is used, still
moistening it with a sponge.

When a Marble veined with several colors is to be
imitated, the different colors of the Marble are separately diluted in weak, warm glue; pastes are made
of each of these shades; they are then flattened down
and placed oue above another, putting those of the
prevailing color of the Marble to be represented, in
the greatest number.   All of these little cakes are
then turned upon the side and cut in slices, which are
immediately spread upon the trowel, care being taken
to direct this trowel, and consequently the colored
materials, in the same direction as that of the Marble
to be imitated.   When the Breccias are copied, pieces
of soft Marbles, such as white and colored alabasters,
are incrusted; these Marbles being rubbed down and
their apparent surfaces polished, present, by reason
of their forms, the usual pebbles of the Breccias.

In general, these coats of impression, which should
be always at least one-fifth of an inch in thickness,
demand much attention and particular pains; for instance, the colors for the surface should be properly
arranged, the glue water should be always warm in
order that the plaster may not set too quickly and
that the rough cast above may be well prepared, etc.

If Etruscan, or other figures are to be made upon

any ground, a pounce is applied when the ground is partly polished; then all the parts which are to receive the incrustations are removed with small chisels, gouges, and other tools suitable for this purpose, and cavities thus formed of from one-fifth to one-eighth of an inch in thickness, according to the outlines designated by the pounce. Small pots are prepared which are filled with the different colors necessary, and of which a paste is made with fine plaster in the palm of the hand, warm glue water being mixed with it; this paste is then introduced in the prepared cavities with a spatula or flexible knife and compactly pressed, the surface being smoothed down as much as possible. If there are several tints, or fillets of light and dark shades, the two edges are scooped out anew in the desired crockets, and the light tints of the reflex and the darker ones forming the shade projected. are applied in the same manner. All the colors suited to this work can be found in commerce.

If, after the termination of the work, any parts of it have not the desired shade, those requiring alteration are pierced again with the etching needle or chisel, and paste inserted of the shade which is wished, care being taken to make these punctures so deep that they will not be rubbed down, and, consequently, effaced, by the polish and the lustre.

Some stucco workers put no plaster in their stuccos, but compound them simply of one part of quick-lime and two parts of pulverized Marble; others mix the quick-lime, powder, and plaster together in equal quantities, and dilute the whole in a glue prepared as for painting upon Marble, but more transparent.

In general, stuccos should be executed in works which are not exposed to dampness, and upon very dry rough-casts of mortar, or plaster, otherwise this humidity repels them, and produces black spots upon the surface of the stucco, or the saltpetre which introduces itself cracks them and causes them to fall.

SECTION THIRD.

OF THE PAINTING UPON, AND THE COLORING OF MARBLES.

OF PAINTING UPON MARBLES.

§ 113. We may be able, by new processes, to facilitate the painting or the coloring of Marbles, but we shall probably never surpass the effects which the ancients obtained, by methods which are now unknown to us.

Upon this point, our tastes differ widely from those of former times, and this is probably owing to the enfranchisement of the people. When the kings held immense numbers of slaves, they could easily undertake those difficult and tedious works, which they could not have imposed upon freemen. The great aim of the slaves was to obey their masters and to satisfy them—the time they counted as little. The great aim of the workmen of the present day is, to provide for their own wants and those of their families; time is every thing to them, and the less of it they employ in the execution of a work, the more they gain thereby.

The painting of the ancients upon Marbles was executed by the same means as the mosaics, in which they employed cubes after having dipped them in colors.

The following process is now in use, according to M. Lisbonne :

" Take a slab of Marble of dimensions analogous to the painting to be made. Commence by properly laying out your design, and, when it is finished, use a sheet of vegetable paper for reversing the tracing ; but in order that it may be more clearly reproduced upon the Marble, rub the under part of this paper with red or black crayon ; then press upon the lines of the drawing as forcibly as possible with a spatula, and the Marble which is to represent the painting will thus receive a good impression. You then, with a brush, surround this design with any wax in a fluid state, but which, when placed on the Marble, will soon solidify. This hinders the acids from spreading over the Marble and defacing it; it also preserves the natural color and polish of those parts of the Marble which bear no design.

§ 114. " Yet, although this process can be used for Marbles which are polished in advance, experience has demonstrated that it is a much better plan to work upon Marbles which have only been rubbed with the pumice-stone, and to which the polish and lustre are not given until the painting has been entirely finished.

" The outline upon the Marble being surrounded with wax, as has just been explained, it is then necessary—in order to complete the cares demanded in this operation, and to give to the design, and, consequently, to the painting, all the necessary distinctness—to rectify the interior; that is, to free it from any wax which may have lodged there, and to cover over any parts, however small, which may need it. This wax would hinder the acid from taking effect, and would render the painting defective.

§ 115. " When these preliminary operations are finished, the acid is poured over the whole surface of the design; the more body required for the painting —that is, the greater the depth of the incrustation which receives it should be—the more acid should be poured on, at intervals calculated according to the effect produced.

" Though there is no general rule given for the depth of the incrustations, this depending upon taste or caprice, they are usually of about the hundredth part of an inch in depth.

§ 116. "In order to pour the acid conveniently upon the design, it should be placed in little cans, specially adapted to dropping it upon every place, whether large or small, which admits the different parts of the design.

"When you have carefully poured over the surface of the design as much acid as is needed to obtain the incrustations, leaving it there for about three minutes in order to produce this effect, you then remove it in the following manner :

"Place the slab of Marble over some vessel, and then, with a sponge filled with clear water, wash the imprints which have received the acid. After this, you remove the wax which had been applied to both the interior and exterior, with a metallic blade, or, which is the better way, by placing the slab of Marble near the fire, which thus receiving a gentle heat, but strong enough to restore the wax to a fluid state, becomes readily cleansed.

"The Marble and the design being thus properly cleansed, the impression of the picture is formed, and you can then proceed to apply the composition, or the different colors suited to give, to the details as well as the whole, a greater or less brilliancy, or an appearance more or less striking, according to the subject to be represented.

"This application of colors can be made either with

the clarified essence of turpentine, the oil of pinks, thick oil, or gummed water, and is executed with the different brushes and pencils ordinarily used by painters.

" When the colors have been tastefully distributed and artistically placed, place the slab of Marble in an ordinary dryer, so arranged as to receive but a temperate heat, but sufficient to properly dry the varied composition with which it has been ornamented ; when it has become sufficiently dry, give the picture several coats of varnish.

" After applying the first coat of varnish, leave it to dry, in order that the second coat may penetrate it better, then give the second and third coats with the proper intervals.

" When the leveling of the painting and Marble is exact and complete, rub the picture with a cushion of wool or cotton wadding, covered with silk or any other smooth and soft tissue. The first rubbing should be forcible, but regular. It is then lightly rubbed over again several times. This operation, which lasts nearly an hour, restores to the painting all the brilliancy which the pumice-stone had destroyed.

" The processes for gilding or silvering the pictures, are analogous to those used in the painting itself.— This additional operation is commenced by forming incrustations with the acid, which may either be made upon certain parts of the picture, or excavated in different portions of the Marble.

These new incrustations permit the attainment of a subdued or burnished gilding, according to the substances and processes employed.

" In the first case, for a subdued gilding, fill the incrustations with a paste composed of calcined white lead and thick oil; then pass over the parts to be gilded or silvered a varnish, composed of gum lac and spirits of wine; apply a coating of oil called *mixture*, composed of old oils and gum resin, dry it, as has been already explained, and when this coating has attained the proper degree of dryness, apply to it the gold or silver leaf, smooth down the metallic leaf upon the mixture, and give to the leaf the coats of varnish necessary to its preservation.

" In the second case, for the burnished gilding, fill the incrustations which have been made upon the painting or Marble, with a red tincture known by the name of *assiette à dorer*, a paste composed of Spanish whiting and strong skin glue or glue for gilding wood.

" Give the incrustations three coats of this red tincture, smooth these down properly, then simply moisten that part of the painting which has been thus covered, with water before applying to it the gold or silver leaf; when this metallic leaf has also been leveled and dried, burnish it with a suitable stone, and give it several coats of varnish.

" In respect to the nature and composition of the acid, colors, and varnish, the best acid is the nitric acid of thirty-six degrees. The colors are those which are usually employed in painting upon wood or canvas, and the varnish used is that of gum copal."

Should we rejoice at, or regret such inventions?— Are these really works of art, or methods of deceiving the public? Experience must answer these questions. The use which may be made of these means of vary- ing the public enjoyments will soon determine their value.

If these paintings are employed upon articles of furniture in common use, they will meet with great success, but wealthy people will always prefer the genuine beauties of Marble, and men of good taste will choose simple ornaments, delicate lines, and de- signs in harmony with the decorations of their apart- ments and the ornamental pieces hanging therein.

ANOTHER PAINTING UPON MARBLE.

§117. Amateurs of mosaics have often been deceived, by showing them paintings imitating mosaic work so closely as to be mistaken for it when not carefully examined. This kind of painting may be made very useful in the ornamenting of certain edifices, stair- ways, peristyles, dining-rooms, baths, and temples for gardens. Marble workers may not often have occa- sion to employ themselves in works of this nature, but they prepare the Marbles on which these paintings are made, and, on this account, we think it advisable to give here the processes for which M. Ciceri, of

Paris, took out a patent of invention for ten years, in September, 1837.

" These new processes," says he, " are designed to replace the use of oil, glue, or of wax, in all kinds of paintings executed upon stone, Marble, stucco, plaster, wood, cartoons, and all porous substances in general.

" The object is to facilitate the execution of ornamental paintings, and to secure their preservation by remedying the inseparable inconvenience of the projection formed upon the marble by the paintings in oil and glue, which will finally grow obscure, because they are not incorporated with the material upon which they are spread."

§ 118. " Before speaking of the different methods of execution upon Marble and other materials," says M. Ciceri, " we will give here the principles of our invention, which consists in the idea of applying to porous substances in order to paint and ornament them, acids, alkalies, alcohols, ethers, etc., containing simple or composite coloring matters in solution or suspension. We will add that these matters, which can be used simply, or mixed with the substances performing the functions of a mordant, act in such a manner as to incorporate themselves with the body, the surface of which is painted ; and that this substance can afterwards be rubbed and polished without effecting the painting. It can also receive a coat of varnish, which forms an imperceptible thickness upon the body thus painted.

" To demonstrate better the novelty, advantages and nature of our process, we will give an example of its application.

" Take a piece of Marble pumiced and softened, either upon its sawed front or a cut surface, and stopped up and coated as if for polishing or painting; then take black ink (tannate of iron,) red ink, (Brazil wood,) rose ink, (cochineal,) and blue ink, (sulphate of indigo,) paint the marble with a common brush, dry it, and then polish it in the usual manner.

" The polishing can be replaced by a varnish upon a sizing put on after the painting, or by a coating of oil applied either cold or warm.

" In both these methods, these coatings of oil, sizing and varnish will deteriorate, as will every preparation of this kind when applied to Marble; while the painting executed by our process will always remain the same by reason of its indelibility, and can never be destroyed since it is absorbed by the Marble into the pores of which it has been introduced.

" This example will suffice to show the conditions of preparation necessary to the colors which we employ, because, if, on one hand, it is necessary that their fluidity should be such as to enable them to penetrate into the pores of the material; on the other, it must not be so great as to allow them to spread like a drop of oil falling upon a porous body; in which case they would no longer be subject to the guidance of the brush.

" These colors should have a sufficient degree of tenuity to prevent the occurrence of these inconveniences; these inks which we employ offer to us this normal condition.

" It should also be observed that, the materials upon which this kind of painting is executed being more or less porous, the coloring substances should possess a degree of tenuity relative to the same degree of porosity."

While leaving to M. Ciceri the entire responsibility of his statements, we cannot but applaud his experiments and the results obtained. and we recommend to Marble workers to endeavor to improve the art and to popularize the use of paintings upon Marble and stone. This may become a new branch of art which will be in great demand in our commerce with foreign countries, as well as for home consumption.

COLORING BY ABSORPTION.

§ 119. The coloring of Marbles by the absorption of colors, which some inventors have recommended as a novelty, has long been successfully practised in Italy, and the following results obtained.

It has been discovered that the solution of nitrate of silver penetrates Marble, giving it a deep red color.

That the solution of nitrate of gold produces a violet color, shading upon purple.

That the solution of verdigris penetrates the Marble deeply, communicating to it a bright green color.

That those of dragon's blood and gamboge also pen-strate it; the first producing a beautiful red, and the other, a yellow color.

That the absorptions may be complete in the above instances it is first necessary, the Marble being well polished, to dissolve the gums and resins in warm alcohol. All the dyes obtained by alcohol from Brazil and Campeachy wood and others, also penetrate the Marble deeply.

It has also been discovered that the tincture of cochineal, prepared in this manner with the addition of a little alum, gives to the Marble a most beautiful scarlet color, penetrating nearly the eighth of an inch. This strongly resembles the African Marble.

The artificial orpiment, or sulphuret of arsenic, dissolved in ammonia, will communicate to the Marble a yellow color in a few moments, which will grow more vivid by exposure to the air.

To all the substances employed for this purpose we should add white wax, mixed with the coloring matters and melted together.

If verdigris is boiled in wax and the mixture laid upon the Marble with an instrument, and afterwards removed from the surface when cold, it will be found that the design has penetrated one-third of an inch, producing a fine emerald color.

We shall enter into some details respecting the execution of this work. When several colors are to be used in succession without confounding them or affecting the clearness of the design, it is necessary to proceed in the following manner.

The tinctures obtained by the spirits of wine and oil of turpentine should be employed upon the Marble while it is hot, particularly when delicate designs are executed; but the dragons' blood and gamboge should be applied to the cold Marble; for this they must be dissolved in alcohol, and the solution of gamboge first used.

This, which is quite clear, grows turbid in a short time, and produces a yellow precipitate, which is used for obtaining a more vivid color; the parts sketched are then heated by passing a plate of red hot iron— or, which is better, a saucepan filled with burning coals —over the surface of the Marble, at the distance of three-fourths of an inch from it. It is then left to cool, after which the parts which the color has not penetrated are heated in the same manner. When the yellow coloring is finished, the solution of dragons' blood is applied in the same manner, and while the Marble is hot, the other vegetable tinctures that do not require a great heat in order to penetrate the Marble, may also be applied. The design is finally completed with the colors mixed with wax; much care is necessary in the application of these, since the least degree of heat beyond the proper point will cause them to spread, for which reason they are less suitable for delicate designs.

These colors should only be applied to the places

where they are designed to remain. Fresh water should be thrown on them from time to time during the operation.

These colors do not impair that of the Marble, which should be well polished before subjecting it to these operations; it is better to use but few colors. Two or three will generally be found sufficient.

We made the assertion at the beginning of this essay, that this art of coloring Marble was not a new invention. Indeed, the ancients understood the incorporation of colors into calcareous substances. Zosimus thus expresses himself on the subject:

"The Marbles are polished to render them more susceptible to the reception and absorption of colors which are then applied. The operation is finished by placing a mordant upon these colors, which preserves the painting, and attaches it so closely to the Marble that both form a part of the same body."

There is also found—

First, in the *Nouvelles Economiques*, vol. xxx., p. 146, published in 1759, an extract from a paper read by the Count de Caylus, in the public session of the Royal Academy of Belles Lettres, on the twenty-fourth of April of the same year, which contains interesting details respecting *A new method of incorporating colors into Marble, and of fixing the sketch.*

Second, in the *Journal Economique*, 1758, p. 169, *A method for penetrating the interior of Marble in such a manner as to be able to paint upon the surface things seeming to be within.* •

Thanks to the progress of chemistry, we may be able to find means of simplifying, and, perhaps, of perfecting this work, but we should not regard as an invention what is often merely an improvement. We can easily infer from all that we have said, that a Marble worker who will study all that has been said upon Marble, and will occupy himself with the application of the processes described, will be able to imitate the finest Marbles, and to enrich this art, which has so long been neglected.

SECTION FOURTH.

OF ARTIFICIAL MARBLES.

§120. Should we commend the efforts which are made to give us counterfeit productions, or ought we to oppose all such products as encouraging fraud, and injuring honorable artists? This is a delicate question when asked respecting jewelry, cloths, furniture, and many other articles. It also affects Marble working, for it is very evident that the artificial Marbles injure the Marble workers, as much as the manufacture of paste jewels injures the diamond merchants.

Notwithstanding this, if the artificial Marble should

become a principal article of commerce, the Marble workers would be better able than any speculators to manufacture Marble, and convert it into a branch of their art. For this reason, we deem it advisable to occupy some time with these artificial Marbles, the success of which is somewhat problematical.

The Marble composed by man has long been known by the name of stucco. Will the artificial Marble be preferable to this? This is doubtful. Will it be more valuable than the plated Marble? Experience must demonstrate it. While waiting for the decision, we will examine the different methods which have been proposed in the course of a few years, and view their respective advantages.

§ 121. In 1823, the first patent of invention was taken out for fifteen years, by Madame Dutillet, for processes relating to the formation of artificial Marble. The following statement was made by her of the discovery which she claimed to have made:

"The artificial Marble which is composed by the aid of calcareous substances, has all the ductility, polish, frigidity, etc., of the natural Marble.

"It can be used for basins, floorings of bath-rooms, vestibules, etc.; in short, in all places which are exposed to drought or humidity. It can also be employed in the construction of churches and other public buildings which dampness defaces, and frescoes can be applied to it with great facility, as the colors do not fade, and retain all their brilliancy."

COMPOSITION OF ARTIFICIAL MARBLE.

§ 122. " To one hundred and ten pounds avoirdupois of pulverized Marble which has been sifted, add thirty-nine pounds of crushed and sifted bricks, and twenty-two pounds of glass, also pounded and sifted. Add to this five times the quantity of hydraulic lime, and carefully stir it with water to form a paste susceptible of being worked with the trowel."

When a smooth layer has been applied to the surface to be coated, draw with a brush the veins and the color of the Marble which you wish to imitate. Then put one pound of Venice talc in a linen cloth, thus forming a packet, and sprinkle the surface that has just been coated and painted. After this gloss it, by rubbing it with the trowel, until the polish and frigidity shall be attained.

" You can give to the paste the color which is to be communicated to the ground of the Marble. For this, add the color at the moment of mixing the paste, taking care only to employ mineral colors. Vegetable colors must never be used.

" A powder may be made of crushed porcelain, silex, sandstone, and other hard stones, or even with clay, (taking care to extract all vegetable matter,) which will amalgamate well with the composition of artificial Marble."

Madame Dutillet seems to have been successful, as

she sold her patent, and the purchaser took out, in 1824, a patent of improvement, in which the following modifications are found

§ 123. The materials employed, as has been said before, must be freed from all vegetable and animal matter which they may contain, that they may form an indestructible composition. After the substances have been pulverized, they are baked long enough to destroy any vegetable or animal parts, and this powder is mixed with thick lime, or hydraulic lime, according to the dampness or nitrifying of the localities. All the colors employed are also purified by fire.

Before applying the material upon the stone, the surface of it should be washed with water, and scraped if necessary; after which, any vegetable matter which may exist upon the stone is destroyed by the means of acids, applied with a brush of amianthus, or mountain flax. Ornaments, and even figures, may be painted by the aid of an economical process, consisting in the use of plates of copper, or of waxed cartoons, which are cut out to form the necessary holes.

When the coatings are finished, and the painting is applied to the Marble or the ornaments, it is polished in the ordinary manner. But, to obtain a greater brilliancy, a composition of the essence of turpentine and white wax melted by the fire, may be used.

This composition is laid upon the surface with a brush, and then rubbed with a skin; and in this way, the essence having consumed all foreign substances which may have lodged on the surface, the wax unites with the material by the action of the lime, and a most beautiful polish is attained.

This new material can also be molded into all kinds of ornaments in relief, busts, statues, chimney-pieces, etc.

§ 124. The matter did not rest here. On the 28th of January, 1825, the patentees of Madame Datillet took out a new patent of addition, in which it is stated that calcareous matters, oyster shells, marl, and talc, should be calcined in a crucible or oven, and then reduced to powder, to which is added an equal part of hydraulic lime, slaked by immersion or otherwise.— The whole should be passed through a silken sieve; and when the composition is to be molded, it should be tempered like plaster. The inventor adds that the polish is obtained by means of Venice talc, and that the coloring can also be laid on the paste.

§ 125. Another process was described in June, 1840, by M. Chenard, of Paris, for which he took out a patent for five years. We will let him speak in his own behalf:

1. " I make a preparation, composed of good linseed oil reduced and the essence of turpentine, which I mix with litharge and umber when the oil is of an inferior quality.

2. " I spread this preparation upon the surface to be marbled, either with a brush or with a metal scraper.

3. " I then dry the article thus coated.

4. " I give it a second coat of the said preparation, and even a third if the body which I wish to Marble is not sufficiently covered by the first and second; a thing which may be easily known if the surface of the body can yet be seen in spite of the coatings already applied. The true ground of the Marble is placed upon these preparatory coatings, the color of which it is to be formed being mixed with it.

5. " I have a trough filled with water, and larger than the object to be marbled, on which I throw the color ground up with the varnish of linseed oil, weaker than that used in the preparation, to which the essence of turpentine and a little table oil is added.

6. " With the breath and a small stick, I arrange this thick substance upon the water in such a manner as to give to the foreign body which I afterwards dip in it, all the different shades, designs, and peculiarities which are found in nature.

7. " I then dip the foreign body, coated with the first preparation, and well dried, in the trough, and draw it forth again ornamented with veins and shades, naturally arranged, which the most skillful painter could not reproduce, since this is a simple effect of nature, while his would be but an incorrect copy.

8. " I then give it a coat of fine varnish, or two if necessary—it being understood that it should be thoroughly dried after each operation, before commencing the following one.

9. " Finally, to obtain the smoothness and appearance of genuine Marble, I give a polishing stroke to the whole, which neither impairs the brilliancy of the colors, or affects the surface to which the composition has been applied."

§ 126. Three years later, M. Riotet made farther discoveries in this art. His idea was to veneer with artificial Marble as a substitute for rosewood, mahogany, and citron wood, both for the inside of boxes, dressing and night tables, and the top of various articles of furniture; besides which, he composed an artificial mosaic, which he calls Parisian mosaic. He makes the following statement of a process which he claims to be both simple and economical :

" Substitute for slabs of natural Marble, those of the artificial Marble, of equal solidity and somewhat less weight. Increase the beauty of the article manufactured by the variety of colors which this artificial Marble may be made to assume, and, above all, by the application of a genuine mosaic, designed with all the art which is used in the composition of mosaics upon stone. This is the object which I have had in view, and which I have finally been permitted to attain.

" The composition which I use for the manufacture of artificial Marble designed for veneering, and for the fabrication of the mosaic, is a mixture. The two substances, when united, acquire a great solidity; the gum arabic diminishes the excessive draught of the gelatine during the drying process and the cabinet work ; in a word, by the union of these two substances, a complete substitute for Marble is obtained in all its applications to veneering, and also to the fabrication of articles of furniture, dressing-cases, ornamental clocks, etc."

COMPOSITION OF THE SLABS OF MARBLE.

Weigh equal quantities of gum arabic and gelatine, hydrate each separately, only softening the gelatine enough to render it entirely flexible.

Place the gum arabic entirely in solution in the smallest possible quantity of water; when it is dissolved, strain it through a coarse cloth in order to separate all foreign substances.

When both are thus prepared, melt the gelatine in a porcelain vessel placed in a water-bath, leave it to boil until a species of skin produced by the scum which , the gelatine always contains is formed upon the surface of the liquid.

During the boiling of the gelatine, prepare the different colors which are to shade and to form the veins and coloring of the Marble.

These colors should be fine, and ground in water ; those most used are silver leaf, white lead, chrome yellow, carmine lake, English green, and all the colors which are generally found in commerce—the gum and gelatine receiving them all.

These different colors are ground in water, and placed separately in vessels designed for this purpose.

PREPARATION FOR CASTING THE SLABS.

§ 127.   The slabs of Marble are cast upon a polished Marble of an inch and a half in thickness and about thirty-five inches square, which is placed upon a strong wooden frame resembling a table; care being taken to place this Marble upon a perfect level, so that the material in running, may be of an equal thickness.

Spread a little suet over the Marble to prevent the adhesion of the material.

The Marble being thus prepared, place a wooden frame of about one-third of an inch in thickness upon it, to receive and retain the material when it is cast.

As regards the size of this frame, supposing that slabs of twenty-five inches square are wished, it will only be necessary to cast them twenty-one or two inches, for, in the succeeding operation of tanning, the slabs will expand three or four inches which will give them the desired size.

As so slender a frame will not rest well upon the Marble, it should be supported by thick wooden wedges, clasped with a cabinet maker's hand screw.

CASTING.

§ 128.   When a slab of Marble of four colors, yellow, green, black and white, is to be made; after the gelatine is boiled and the gum is well dissolved, take a sufficient quantity of each of these colors to color a quart in the whole of the gum and gelatine used in the operation, place these separately in small earthen pans, take the solution of gum, and pour an equal quantity in each of these pans in order to dilute the colors, (care being taken that every particle of color is diluted,) then take the gelatine, which must be strained through a cloth to make it clear, and pour the same quantity into the pans in which the colors have been diluted with the gum. Stir the whole well with a brush, that the mass may be well mixed and the color uniformly distributed through the liquid, let it rest for a few moments in order to give the bubbles of air which have formed during the agitation, time to come to the surface; then remove these with a skimmer until the liquid is entirely free from them: This is very important in obtaining smooth slabs of Marble. When this has been done, pour these four different colors into a vessel especially designed for this purpose, and which may be described as resembling four funnels joined together, the tubes resting against each other.

It can be easily understood that, on leaving the orifice of each of these tubes, the colors mix and unite in spreading over the Marble, thus forming the rich and varied shades of the finest Marbles, lapis, porphyry, etc.

This may be done in a different manner when imitations of ribboned stones are wished. For this, pour each of the colors separately upon the Marble, taking care to spread them in small pools over the whole surface; then, with a wooden spatula, form the ribboned shades which are wished, by lightly moving the mixture.

In both these operations, the last in particular, it is impossible to prevent the formation of bubbles of air in the agitation. The best method of destroying them is, after the material has congealed, to take a fine wet sponge, and burst these bubbles by gently striking them. When this has been done, take a thin plate of sheet iron about twelve inches square, with the edges raised in such a manner as to hold burning coals; pass this over the surface, as near to it as possible without touching the material.

This intense heat will melt the surface of the slab, and close the vacuum formed by the bubbles of air.

TANNAGE OF THE SLABS OF MARBLE.

§ 129. The most important operation in the composition of artificial Marbles is that of tannage, without which it would be impossible for the cabinet maker to scrape and polish the material. It would be too malleable for any use.

It is very evident that a soluble matter like the gelatine and gum would melt by the heat caused by the scraper and cling to it in particles, in which case instead of smoothing them, the tool would produce a contrary effect.

The result of this tannage is, to render the gum and gelatine insoluble, even in boiling water, and to transform it into a substance resembling horn. In this state, indeed, the material is scraped and polished in the same manner as horn.

§ 130. For this operation, a tank lined with lead of about twenty-seven inches in length, and fifty in breadth is required, as room is necessary to change the place of the slabs which are placed in it.

This tank is designed for the reception of the liquid possessing the property of tanning.

This liquid is composed of one part of the sulphate of alumina based on potash, and twenty parts of water.

Pour this liquid into the tank, and place the slabs in it, leaving them until their entire thickness is thoroughly penetrated by the liquid. To be sure of this, by cutting off a small corner it can be seen how far it has penetrated, that part which has absorbed the liquid will present a shining appearance, while that which is not penetrated will be of a dull color.

. When the liquid has entirely penetrated the slabs, draw them from the tank, wash them in clear water and wipe them carefully; then fix them on strong wooden frames by the aid of very strong plaits of thread coated with glue. Glue a light cloth upon the frame in such a manner as to sustain the weight of the slabs during the drying process, and then expose them to

the open air upon benches, leaving space enough between them to permit the air to circulate freely.

When the drying is complete, moisten the cloth and
plaits that hold the slab in the frame, carefully, in
order to avoid breaking the slabs.

FABRICATION OF MOSAICS.

§ 131. This composition of gum and gelatine can
not only be made to assume the form and appearance
of Marble, but with small fillets of various colors,
ornamental work, such as mosaic, may also be obtained.

The different experiments which I have made convince me that one could, by my process, attain the
perfection of the ancient mosaics; this would be of
great importance to many of the arts, such as jewelry,
bronze, and cabinet work in particular, in which nothing of the kind has ever been known.

It is easy to imagine the effect which a mosaic of
flowers or any other design would produce upon an
article of furniture.

Until the present time, mosaic work has kept many
amateurs at a distance by its high price. By my process it can be easily used in various arts, since a diminution of at least four-fifths of its price is procured.

To make a boquet of flowers, or a rose, for instance,
the design must first be executed in water colors by a
skillful artist. This design is then divided into
squares like the patterns for needle-work. By this

means this rose will be divided into at least a thousand little squares containing all the shades. These squares traced on the design show the number of fillets necessary to the formation of the rose, these being shaded precisely like the design.

By joining these square fillets together, the model will be exactly reproduced.

For the fabrication of these fillets, slabs of plain colors should be made by the process which I have just described for the Marble.

§ 132. In executing a design, it is important to study carefully the shades of each flower. It is evident that at least six shades are needed to form the rose; namely, white, which forms the light, light rose, rose, deep rose, red, and dark red which gives the shade.

Proceed in the same manner for all other flowers of different colors.

When the different colored slabs which are needed in the composition of the mosaic are dry, remove them from the frames in the manner which I have just described for the Marble. Soak them in the trough in pure water for about a quarter of an hour until they are flexible, then place the slab thus moistened between two blocks of wood so that the surface may be entirely covered, leave it thus for twelve hours in order to give the water time to penetrate it thoroughly and then proceed to the cutting of the fillets.

For this operation in which the fillets should all

be of the same size, this regularity can only be obtained by a fillet-cutter, formed with precision.

GLUEING OF THE FILLETS TO FORM THE DESIGN.

§ 133. When the design is to be formed by the collection of the fillets, the design which is divided into squares must be used.

We will suppose this design to be divided in one direction in fifty lines, which are themselves crossed by fifty others, thus giving a total of two thousand five hundred fillets; these fillets should be glued in straight lines of fifty fillets each, calculating the shades which should compose them from the pattern, with the aid of a tool designed to keep the fillets in place while they are being glued.

When the rows have been thus glued and carefully numbered, they should be placed upon each other, according to their numbers, in such a manner as to form a block, which should be surrounded with strong paper or thin wood in order that the fillets may not be unglued in cutting this block in slices.

UNCHANGEABLE CHINESE PAINTINGS.

§ 134. These paintings are executed upon paper, and covered over with a very transparent and well tanned sheet of gum and gelatine, prepared by the same process as the slabs of artificial Marble.

When the drying process is complete, scrape one side of the sheet with a cabinet maker's scraper until it is perfectly smooth. Then detach it from the frame and cut it in the shape and size of the articles which it is to cover.

Use gum arabic dissolved in water for the application of the designs; spread a coating of it over the transparent sheet, lay on the design and glue it by means of a strong pressure under a press.

One important precaution should be taken in order that the glue used by the cabinet maker in veneering, may not penetrate through the paper; namely, to spread a coating of strong glue upon the side which is to be veneered, afterwards sprinkling it with well dried Bougival white by means of a silken sieve. This operation should be repeated twice at least; it is then left to dry, and afterwards inlaid in veneerings and cuttings.

§ 135. The provinces also endeavored in 1842, to produce artificial Marbles. M. Mondon, of Vienna, claimed to have found a material suitable for this purpose in the department of Charente. He calls it *gypseous alabaster*—a soft substance which must first be hardened in the following manner :

Put the pieces to be worked in a furnace, placed upon sheets of zinc, which are formed in such a manner as to hold water. This furnace should be built so that the pieces may not come in contact with the fire; leave them for an hour exposed to the action of a heat not strong enough to bake them, for this substance being gypseous, they would thus be reduced to baked plaster and would have no solidity. When the material is well heated and freed from all humidity, the pieces should be sprinkled with tepid water in which a quantity of alum, proportioned to the number of pieces, has been dissolved ; they may even be soaked in it for a moment. The tepid water which has not been absorbed by the material is then removed, and cold water is placed in them.

By this means they attain such a degree of hardness, that the final polish can only be given after successively using the sand-stone, pumice-stone, and shave-grass ; care being taken to constantly sprinkle the piece, as it will otherwise be impossible to polish it ; lastly, a little white wax is spread upon a linen cloth, and, by rubbing with this, the finest white Marble is obtained.

The colored Marbles are made in the same manner, with the exception of the dissolution of the color wished for the Marble in the water which is used to harden it, using Campeachy wood for the red, indigo for the blue and white Marble, etc.

§ 136. M. Buisson of Bordeaux, also took out a patent on the 14th of December, 1842. He gives the following recipe.

A block of eighty inches in length and twenty-five in width, should be placed in a sheet iron basin about three feet in depth, and somewhat longer and broader than the block. Place this basin in a kiln heated to twenty-eight degrees, and maintain the same degree of heat for five hours.

At the end of this time, fill the basin with boiling water in which a solution of two and one-fifth pounds of common alum in twelve quarts of water has first been poured.

The basin should be kept filled with the same water for seventy-two hours, a gentle heat being maintained in the kiln, in order that the block of Marble may become thoroughly impregnated, and acquire the hardness of Marble.

The Cognac plaster produces statuary Marble of the greatest purity.

The Rouen plaster produces the same, but with less whiteness.

For Marbles of two and a half inches in thickness for fronts of buildings, mantels of chimney pieces, pavements, etc., the same process is used, but the plaster stones must first be sawed to the required dimensions and placed in the basin at the distance of two inches apart, and baked for five hours in the kiln heated to the degree we have mentioned, after which, water prepared in the manner before described is poured upon them, and the whole is left undisturbed for twenty-four hours.

§ 137. In order to obtain different tints, the following drugs are dissolved in the alum water.

For black; four-fifths of a grain, Troy weight, of *bulaque*, three-tenths of a grain of verdigris, and as much copperas, in twelve quarts of water and two and one-fifth pounds of alum, avoirdupois.

For rose; three and a half pints of the decoction of old Brazil wood, in twelve quarts of water, and two and one-fifth pounds of alum.

For yellow; two and one-fifth pounds avoirdupois of woad or dyers' weed, in the above quantity of alum water.

SECTION FIFTH.

OF TERRACES.

§ 138. If Marble workers confined themselves to working upon Marble alone, we should deem it unnecessary to give practical instructions concerning the construction of antique areas, or pavements of terraces. But they often have to execute works which properly belong to the province of stone cutters, in which they do not succeed, either for want of proper foundations on which to work, or because they have not good materials, or for want of mastics solid enough to resist the inclemency of the seasons. It is therefore of the greatest importance, that they should be placed in possession of information which may enable them to overcome the obstacles with which they have to contend.

Vitruvius, after having spoken of the stuccos of his time and described their composition, said that they made use of similar methods to form areas upon terraces in courtyards and apartments. Before the composition had dried, they incrusted small pieces of colored Marble in it to ornament it. Sometimes they only mixed crushed tile with the coating, which gave it the appearance of a kind of red granite, and also increased its solidity. This last composition was called *opus signinum*, from the city of Signia, celebrated for the excellence of its tiles.

§ 139. The art of constructing areas of the pavements of terraces, says M. Hericart de Thury, being now nearly lost or forgotten, it is very desirable to find some one sufficiently versed in the theory and practice of this art to draw up some elementary instructions, designed to enlighten workmen in respect to the principles of the ancients in relation to the construction of antique areas.

§ 140. M. Laudier, former chief of the engineering batallion, in his campaigns had closely studied the antique areas and the pavements of Venetian terraces, and has employed his leisure in preparing an elementary treatise upon this subject. We shall extract from this whatever information may be useful to Marble workers, masons, and stone cutters.

CHAPTER FIRST.

PREPARATION OF THE AREA.

OF THE FIRST COATING.

§ 141. Pavements and Venetian terraces are built in apartments, ground floors, over vaults, and upon frame work covered with boards, not only in covered places but also in the open air. In all cases the manner of constructing them is precisely the same; care must be taken, however, in laying the first coating upon a ground floor, that the plane surface should be dry and the earth well trod down and perfectly level.

When this is done, the overseer of the work draws marks in the angles of the apartment, two inches from the ground, and then, with a rule, connects these marks by a thick, black line. This ground is then covered with the first coating, consisting of old plaster, work and bricks, which is spread over it smoothly and pressed down to the height of the black mark. This is then again compressed with the beetle, and is moistened with lime water during this operation by means of small brooms.

To level this mass, the rule and level are used.

OF THE SECOND COATING.

§ 142. Another black line is drawn around the apartment, about three inches above the first. This line determines the thickness of the second coating, which is also composed of plaster work and old bricks, prepared in the following manner: the plaster work and bricks are first pounded together, and then mixed with lime and sand, thus forming a thick mortar.

When a sufficient quantity of the mortar has been prepared, it is laid on the first coating to the thickness of three inches, this mass is then spread over the surface and harrowed with an iron rake, and is then smoothed with a lath, the level being used. It is then moistened with lime water and compressed again with the beetle, pounded with an iron rammer until the coating resembles a wall freshly plastered, and finally pressed down again with the beetle. When this second coating is nearly dry, the third, called the red coating, is applied.

COMPOSITION OF THE RED COATING.

§ 143. For this purpose, old or new tiles are pounded, and then passed through a coarse sieve; when a sufficient quantity has thus been prepared, it is put in heaps, after first separating any pieces that may have mixed with it.

To make the mixture, two heaps are formed, one

containing two-thirds of the crushed bricks, and the other one-third of lime; these are thrown by alternate shovelfulls into a third heap, thus amalgamating the bricks and lime; this dry mass is then turned over with an iron rake until it is thoroughly mixed.

When this has been turned several times, it is sprinkled with water, and then stirred again with the rake, until it has acquired the consistency of partially compact mortar; which it will soon do if the tiles were well dried when mixed.

MANNER OF APPLYING THE RED COATING.

§ 144. The mortar is spread over the surface in the manner before described. This coating should be from two to two and a half inches in thickness. If the second coating is found too dry to yield to the red mortar and to properly unite with it, the whole floor must be sprinkled, and when the surface is sufficiently moistened, the mortar is thrown on it in heaps, and then evenly spread over with the iron rake.

In ordinary cases, the rule and level are applied to every part of the room, and the whole is carefully leveled. The whole thickness of the three coatings, particularly in rooms upon the ground floor where dampness is to be feared, should be from seven to eight inches; it is a good plan to arrange little trenches by which the water can run off.

When the leveling is finished, the whole surface

should be consolidated and made perfectly smooth with the iron beetle.

The leveling, in this part of the work, is made in the following manner:

When the red mass is spread out, a well planed lath, which should be as long as the width of the room, is laid upon the ground. Two workmen, each in the corner of the apartment, place this lath lengthwise, and then, by drawing it along, always keeping it on the same level, they remove the surface of the mortar, constantly applying the level in order to secure a perfect leveling.

The coating of mortar being thus perfectly leveled, it is beaten with the iron rammer and the beetle. The red mortar in the corners of the room should be beaten as soon as spread on, as it dries much sooner than that in the middle.

OF THE FOURTH COATING

§ 145. A white coating is spread over the red coat which is called *lo stabilido* or *il bianco;* this coating is prepared in the following manner:

A quantity of white or greyish marble is pounded into small fragments, or rather grains, which are then passed through a sieve of iron wire, fine enough to only permit the passage of that resembling coarse sand. Two parts of this coarse sand is then mixed with one part lime, and the whole is amalgamated until it acquires the consistency of a stiff mortar, which is called by the workmen, *il bianco.*

OF THE APPLICATION OF THE MARBLE MORTAR.

§ 146. When a sufficient quantity of the Marble mortar has been prepared, it is placed in a trough and carried into the room in which the pavement is made, and then spread over the red coating in the following manner :

A workman with a mason's trowel throws the mortar in small heaps in straight lines, about three inches apart ; a second workman then spreads them evenly over the whole surface of the floor with a round steel trowel.

The thickness of this coating of Marble mortar should be from three to three and a half inches.

Any color that may be wished may be given to this mortar, by using yellow, green, or any other colored Marble; but white Marble is usually preferred, as the designs appear to better advantage on it, as well as the pieces of Marble.

When the coating of white mortar begins to dry, the design should be lightly traced upon it; after which the second part of the process begins, which consists in applying the different colored Marbles needed to compose the design which has been traced.

CHAPTER SECOND.

WORKING OF THE MARBLE.

METHOD OF BREAKING THE MARBLE.

§ 147. While part of the workmen are employed in laying down the first, second, third, and fourth coatings, another workman sorts the different colors of Marble suitable to the design. Fragments of old, broken Marbles, which are no longer of use, will serve for this purpose. Indeed they are those best suited to this kind of work, since one side of them is polished. In respect to those used for the mortar, their form is indifferent, since they are only used after having been crushed.

The different sorts of Marbles are broken with a mallet into small pieces, the largest of which should not exceed two and a half or three inches in length and as many in width, and with no regularity of form; these are then thrown in heaps according to their colors.

These heaps are next passed through a large iron sieve, in order to separate the large and small pieces, thus forming two distinct portions.

When all the outlines of the design have been traced on the floor, and the color of each of them has been decided, the workmen commence by making framings of small pieces of Marble of a suitable color, which they fit in the mass with as much regularity as possible, taking care always to place their largest side on the line of the design, and the irregular sides within the framing.

When these little pieces are properly placed, the workman presses them down with his thumb, continuing through the lines in this manner before proceeding to the inside of the framing, which does not demand the same regularity.

OF THE APPLICATION OF THE MARBLE.

§ 148. For this process, the workman fills his apron pockets with pieces of the different colored Marbles needed in the design ; he then kneels, and, following the outline of the design, presses the small pieces of Marble with his thumb exactly side by side, in the partially softened mass which forms the fourth coating.

The framing of the design being formed with these pieces, which should be as nearly as possible of the same size, he proceeds to the inlaying of the centre ground, commonly called *the mirror.*

When the mirror contains no design, he simply takes pieces of Marble of what should be the prevailing color ; or, what is better, he uses Marbles of different colors, which produces a beautiful effect.

MANNER OF PAVING THE MIRROR.

§ 149. The pieces of the kind and color of Marbles which should prevail in the mirror should be larger than the others, and also as flat as possible; the workman spreads them over the floor, leaving them to be arranged by chance, only taking care that they shall not be too close together.

The mirror being covered, all those pieces should be laid flat which, in falling, took some other position, or turned their polished side downwards. To place them in this manner the workmen use several planks, upon which they kneel and thus advance, working directly before them.

These large fragments, flatly placed at a proper distance from each other, give the prevailing color to the mirror. After this, all the spaces between the large fragments are filled up with smaller pieces of different colored Marbles; such as white, red, yellow black, reddish, greenish, etc., thus forming a mixture of colors beautifully shaded.

To ascertain whether the colors produce a good effect, the part which is finished is sprinkled with a broom dipped in water; this draws forth all the brilliancy of the colors.

The floor being paved in the manner described, the pressure by the stone cylinder next succeeds.

USE OF THE STONE CYLINDER.

§ 150. Before using this cylinder, the whole floor should be well sprinkled with water, so that not only the white coating may be softened, but also the red mortar which is beneath it. This being done, the cylinder should be carefully placed, so as not to disarrange the small pieces of Marble, and first rolled over the edge of the mirror nearest the door. The work should always commence at this point, in order to avoid the effacing of the drawing in going in and out.

The cylinder rolls forward and backward, and the place over which it passes should be well sprinkled frequently with water.

The corners of the casements, and all places which cannot be reached with the cylinder, should be pressed with the beetle, and beaten down with the iron rammer.

When the cylinder has been rolled long enough to force the small pieces of Marble deeply into the red coating, so that it can be perceived that the white mass begins to form a kind of coat, and that the whole is sufficiently incrusted, it is again pressed down with the beetle, and smoothed over with the iron rammer.

USE OF THE SMALL POLISHER.

§ 151. The coating of Marble having been well rolled by the cylinder, pressed down and beaten, and sunk to the red mass, leaving only the coat of white mortar visible upon the surface; the workmen commence polishing in every direction with the small polisher.

For the recesses of the windows and all other places in which the small polisher cannot be used, the workman uses a piece óf hone or coticular stone large enough to be grasped with both hands, with which he polishes all the corners of the apartment, also filling up all interstices which may have formed.

In proportion as the surface is polished, a workman supplied with a trowel, a hod filled with white Marble mortar, and various small pieces of Marbles, fills up the empty spaces, and sinks new pieces where they are wanting; he then sprinkles the place, and passes the polisher over it. The Marble mortar which is forced out by the sprinkling and polishing, is in a liquid state; this the workman removes with a steel trowel, forcibly scraping the part until nothing more remains on the surface.

FORCING DOWN THE LARGE PIECES OF MARBLE.

§ 152. When the mirror is entirely inlaid with large pieces of Marble, some of which are found to rise above the others, or to be detached from them, they are forced down again with a quadrangular wooden prism. This prism is placed upon the piece of Marble, and the opposite side lightly struck, to sink it.

This coating of natural Marble being smoothed down with the small polisher, leveled and worked with the steel trowel, and a slight degree of polish attained, the large polisher or large grindstone is then used.

USE OF THE LARGE POLISHER.

§ 153. The large polisher consists of a grindstone of twenty inches in diameter, with a part of its cylindrical form removed; it then rests on a flat surface of about two inches, with which the instrument rests upon the pavement; this gives it more effect when set in motion.

This grindstone, being very heavy, should be worked by two men, one holding the polisher very near the head, and the other the middle of the handle.

During this operation the pavement is carefully sprinkled, and the empty spaces which may have formed are filled up with the Marble mortar.

When a very large polisher is used, two men will not be sufficient to work it; a rope is then attached to the front of the grindstone, with which the third workman draws it towards him, while the other two shove it from their side.

When the pavement is sufficiently smoothed by the action of the large polisher, (for the polish is not yet begun,) the work is again commenced in divisions not exceeding twelve superficial feet. Each of these must be worked in every direction for an hour and a half, after which a workman kneeling, with a piece of hone or coticular stone, placed flatly, passes over the part which has just been worked, rubbing it with a circular movement.

The operation of polishing draws out upon the surface of the pavement a liquid matter, arising from the sprinkling and the diluted mortars. When the workman has rubbed sufficiently with the hone, he removes this liquid with the blade of the steel trowel, passing it circularly until the Marble appears to be already half polished.

USE OF THE IRON RAMMER.

§ 154. The preceding work being finished, a workman takes an iron rammer, with which he gently beats the surface, in order that the pieces of Marbles may be forced still deeper into the white and red masses, which are softened by the frequent sprinkling, and unite themselves with the entire mass.

In this operation, as in the preceding one, if any of the small stones have become deranged by the rubbing or pressing down, they should be replaced with the Marble mortar, and forced down with the wooden prism.

The Marble coating of the mirror having been well polished the first time, as has been said before, the same is repeated, using the small polisher for polishing the borders made of the small stones; these are more easily worked than the middle, which requires the use of the large polisher, and more time.

After a second working, a piece of hone is again used for removing the liquid mass drawn out by the polishing, and the surface is scraped with the round trowel. As this mass has become very thin by frequent sprinklings and is no longer of use, it is removed in a bucket, and the pavement is finally beaten with the iron rammer.

THIRD POLISHING.

§ 155. When the pavement is somewhat dry, it is polished again, as in the first and second polishing, and the whole is worked anew with the large grindstone.

FOURTH POLISHING.

§ 156. The same process is repeated for the fourth time, always observing to polish the corners and borders with the small, and the mirror with the large polisher. Not as much time, however, is required for this. The half of that demanded by the previous operations will be sufficient.

This work being finished, the whole pavement is rubbed with wheat bran on a cushion of wool. When this has been sufficiently rubbed, it is swept with a horse hair brush, after which the borders are marked with a black crayon, in order that they may not be passed in applying the color.

PREPARATION OF COLORS AND THEIR USES.

§ 157. The red is simply diluted with water and then applied to the coating of red Marble.

The yellow and green are prepared in the following manner :

Bruise a quantity of juniper berries, and boil them in a few pints of water, then pour off the water from the residuum; this water is used in grinding the green or yellow, which is mixed well with the white mass of the Marble.

The colors thus prepared are laid on the green and yellow borders with a large brush, serving only to color those parts of the mortar visible between the seams of the pieces of Marble forming the last coating; this gives to these mortars the color of the Marbles which are encrusted with them.

In a few days, the colors being well dried, the whole apartment is again cleansed with the bran and a woolen cushion. This final operation produces an apartment wholly paved with perfectly polished Marble, and resembling a most beautiful mosaic.

SUBSEQUENT OPERATION NECESSARY TO PRESERVE AND PERFECT THE PAVEMENT.

§ 158. The entire mass having acquired a perfect dryness and solidity, which takes place in three months, another mortar of fine white Marble is prepared, with which the whole pavement is again covered. This mortar should not be too thick. It is spread with a steel trowel, and the cavities are filled up which have formed during the drying of the pavement. The superfluous mortar is then removed, and, after the whole is well dried, linseed oil is passed over the whole by means of woolen cushions, which produces a fine gloss, and increases the perfection of the work; this operation should be repeated every year.

CHAPTER THIRD.

LESS COSTLY VENITIAN PAVEMENTS.

FIRST METHOD.

§ 159. We offer the following less costly method of constructing pavements, to those who do not wish to incur the expense of those executed in Marble.

The floor of the apartment is first prepared with the first, second, and third coatings, as has been described. Then, instead of spreading upon the red coating, which is the third, the coating of white mortar; after having provided small round and flat pebbles, or any other kinds of broken stones that may be wished, they are spread at hazard over the whole surface of the red coating, taking care thát they may be near enough each other.

They are then rolled with the stone cylinder in the same manner as the Marble pavements, until the stones are forced down into the red coating so as not to appear on the surface.

When, after a few hours, the work commences to

dry, the lines are drawn, necessary to encircle the design which is to be given to the following coating :

This upper coating, which is laid on according to the design, is the same as that designated in the second chapter, under the name of the *mortar of white Marble*, and consists of Marble, pounded and reduced to sand and mixed with lime ; but with the difference that this mass is not white like the first, but of the different colors which have been delineated on the design.

These colored mortars are composed like the white mortars, of green, yellow, red and other marbles, reduced to a kind of coarse sand, and afterwards mixed with lime. They are spread with the steel trowel over the different divisions of the design, according to the colors to be given them; this coating is then pounded with the iron. rammer and leveled with the trowel. This coating of colored mortar should be from an inch to an inch and a half in thickness.

When the floor begins to dry, a coating of its respective color is spread over each division of the design, after which it is cleansed and polished with a woolen cushion. At the end of a few months, the floor is again covered with colored mortars, thinner than the first ; these are spread and carefully smoothed, after which linseed oil is passed over it, and it is polished with bran.

SECOND METHOD.

§ 160. In hotels, restaurants, warehouses, galleries, cellars, and all other places in which a dry and solid floor without ornament is required, the fourth coating of colored Marble is useless; it is sufficient to force down repeatedly the gravel or stone which has been used with the stone cylinder, afterwards consolidating and leveling it with the iron rammer.

THIRD METHOD.

§ 161. Ordinary pavements can also be made by taking common stones and pounding and reducing them to coarse sand, which is then mixed with lime and old plaster stuff. When this mass is well mixed, and has acquired the consistency of a thick mortar, it is spread upon the third or red coating; this layer should be from an inch and a half to two inches in thickness. It is then smoothed and leveled with the cylinder, and pounded with the iron rammer. A stony mass is thus formed, which is solid and impenetrable, and is not impaired by time or temperature.

This pavement may be used in the open air, and upon frame-work as well as terraces, as it is perfectly impervious to water.

In this complicated work, everything depends upon the manner in which the described operations are executed. They have already been sufficiently tested, and, if the work does not succeed, it should be attributed to unskillfulness, and not to the defect of the process. We see daily, bitumen terraces, which are perfectly solid, and others which are imperfect; nevertheless, this rule is as old as civilization, and we owe to it the works which centuries have not been able to destroy. But to this rule, another should succeed, namely :—that work which is well done should be well paid for.

Fifth Part.

MANUFACTURE OF TOY MARBLES,

WAX VARNISH, MOSAIC BY ABSORPTION OF COLORS, ARTIFICIAL MOSAICS, LETTERS FOR INSCRIPTIONS, PAINTINGS—FIGURES IN RELIEF.

THIS part of our Manual is rather a complement of details affecting Marble working than a branch of the art of the Marble worker, yet we have thought it advisable to give it place, lest the public should deem our work incomplete. It treats of the manufacture of toy marbles, of mosaics by absorption of colors, of artificial mosaics, of letters for inscriptions, of paintings upon Marble, of figures in relief, and of the coloring of Marbles. All of these details possess a certain interest, if not for Marble workers, for professional builders, and for amateurs who like to inform themselves concerning certain processes, by which results are obtained which seem to present many more difficulties than they really possess. We will begin with accounts relating to the manufacture of toy marbles.

SECTION FIRST.

MANUFACTURE OF TOY MARBLES.

§ 162. Every manufacture which supplies the wants of numerous purchasers is always sure of finding a rapid sale, and, if the manufactured article is apt to be broken or lost, it is evident that this sale will be greatly increased. This is true respecting the manufacture of toy marbles. It does not properly belong to the special province of the Marble worker, but it is one of the products of the art of Marble working, and is therefore entitled to a place in this little treatise upon the use and manufacture of articles in Marble. We give the following extract from a statement made by a manufacturer of Strasbourg.

The first operation consists in breaking the calcareous mineral into small pieces, proportioned to the size of the marbles which are to be made. This may be done in the quarry, by means of mallets resembling those used by road laborers. These pieces are then sorted and matched in equal sizes.

The second operation consists in removing the roughest asperities of the prepared pieces, thus beginning to give them a round form. During the · time in which the apparatus for rounding prepares one hundred pounds, the apparatus for rough-hewing furnishes one thousand, and the millstone for scraping, two thousand pounds.

§ 163. The operation of scraping is performed by a millstone, set in motion by some moving power; its arrangement does not differ much from those commonly used in flour mills.

The upper or moving millstone is commonly of about one-third less weight than that of ordinary millstones, in order that the pressure may not act too violently upon the asperities of the Marble, and that this millstone may present greater facilities for being raised or lowered at pleasure. For this purpose, the vertical shaft of the millstone should turn in a brass socket.

§ 164. The most convenient dimensions of the millstones are the following:

The stationary millstone should be of twenty-five inches in diameter, and from eight to ten inches in thickness.

The turning millstone, which moves with great velocity, requires nearly or quite the power of two men for ordinary work.

The drum of the millstones is formed by a wooden hoop, four and one-third inches in width, and placed on a level with the upper edge of the stationary millstone which it includes in its circumference: this hoop is itself surrounded with a rim of six and a half inches in height, and is designed to keep back the calcareous matter which the movement of the millstone may throw towards the edges.

§ 165. The third operation (rough-hewing), consists in commencing to round the calcareous matters by means of friction against each other, and also against the cylinders of hard stone: this is done by an apparatus which is composed of a hollow cylinder of hard stone of 3–28 inches in length, and 21–65 inches in diameter; the rim of the cylinder should be 3–14 inches in thickness.

Another cylinder of hard stone of 35–43 inches in length and 6–61 in diameter, having a groove in the middle to admit an iron shaft of 2–16 square inches, also aids in this operation.

The brass trays forming the cylinder are each furnished with a hinge, and have a flange extending into the inside of the cylinder; these trays are attached to the cylinder by two pins and by wooden wedges.

The calcareous materials are introduced into the cylinder through the openings, and the cylinder is moved by a pulley.

§ 166. To obtain the greatest effect the quantity of calcareous matter introduced into the cylinder should not exceed two-thirds of the space between the cylinders.

The proper degree of velocity is from forty to forty-five turns per minute, a greater volocity than this produces the effect of a fly wheel, which makes the substances immoveable, thus depriving them of friction.

The calcareous dust should be thrown out from time to time, as this diminishes the action of the friction if it accumulates in the cylinder.

§ 167.   The fourth operation consists in completely rounding the calcareous materials by the use of another apparatus, composed of a wooden cylinder or cask with a double bottom of 65 inches in length and 52 in diameter.

Also, a cylinder of hard stone, or several cylinders of a total length of 49–21 inches and a diameter of 6–49, with a groove of 2–16 inches in the middle to admit an iron shaft.

The staves of the interior compartment are held back to the trays by a grooving, and those of the outer compartment are confined with pins.

· The calcareous matters are passed through the openings into the first and second compartment of the tray, the velocity of which should equal from forty to forty-five turns per minute.

§ 168.   The following process is employed in proportion to the degree of dead polish wished, and according to the facility of rounding the materials; this, however, is sufficient only for common marbles.

The rounding is obtained solely by friction; all the dust arising from the calcareous matter is then extracted from the cask, and a small quantity of emery in pieces of the size of a bean is mixed with it; this quickly completes the rounding and gives the desired polish.

After the manufactured Marbles are taken from the apparatus, the remainder of the emery may be extracted by the sifting of the dust, for a second use.

About two-thirds of the Marbles have a dead polish, which is attained by the use of these first four processes; the remaining third, which are of white or colored Marbles, have a shining polish, obtained by an additional process.

§ 169. This shining polish is obtained by the process of the friction of the calcareous matters, and by the use of the second apparatus, arranged in the following manner :

The stone cylinder is rejected. In its place, a wooden cylinder covered with zinc, with its compartments also lined with zinc, is used.

After having obtained the perfect roundness and the dead polish described in the fourth operation, the Marbles are placed again in an apparatus not lined with zinc, a small quantity of emery is introduced, and about two hundred turns are given it.

The globes are then taken from this apparatus, and placed again in that lined with zinc. If they are of white Marble, a small quantity of emery dust is mixed with them to complete the polishing.

§ 170. If the globes to be polished are of other Marble, or of shaded, calcareous stone, a small quantity of the powder of calcined tin is introduced into the apparatus. A part of the common Marbles with a dead polish, also consists of colored globes, which take a shining polish by coloring.

§ 171. This sixth process is executed thus:

When the fourth operation is finished, the globes are placed in the apparatus lined with zinc, and the preparations for coloring are poured upon them—not all at once, but from time to time in small quantities, and after having turned the apparatus several times.

When the coloring preparations have adhered to the globes, they are finished by giving them a final polish, which is quickly obtained by introducing a small quantity of the dust of calcined tin into the apparatus.

Despite the difficulty of coloring compact, calcareous substances durably, without heating them, this coloring may be executed both cold and dry, by the use of the following preparations :

For red, take dragons' blood in drops, reduce this gum to powder, and grind it in a glass mortar with spirits of wine or a urinous lixivium

For the manufacture of common globes, the dragons' blood may be used alone without any preparation.

For vermilion, dissolve a quantity of vermilion in urine and quick-lime.

For brown, take pitch mixed with turpentine.

For yellow, use the gum of gamboge, reduced to powder, and ground with spirits of wine in a glass mortar.

For yellow, the extract of saffron, dissolved in urine and quick-lime, may also be used.

For golden yellow, take equal quantities of crude salts of ammonia, white vitriol, and verdigris; grind them together, and when they are reduced to a fine powder, dissolve them in spirits of wine or a urinous lixivium.

For green, use green wax dissolved in a urinous lixivium.

§ 172. Although these processes have been found very successful, the following improvements have lately been effected:

The pieces are roughly rounded by groovings made in the turning millstone. A wooden tray descends until the calcareous pieces just rest in the groovings with which its under surface is furnished, and which correspond exactly with the groovings of the upper surface of the turning millstone.

The depth of the groovings in the turning millstone forms half the diameter of the globes which are to be made; that of the groovings in the wooden tray forming the other half.

The wooden tray is penetrated by a vertical shaft, passing through an aperture arranged in the middle in such a manner that the shaft can turn without touching the tray. This tray can be raised or lowered at will, by a small gear adjusted to a little shaft, which raises the tray by means of two leathern straps rolling round this shaft.

The wooden tray is prevented from turning by means of brass sockets fixed by screws upon the upper part of the tray; these sockets slide in grooves arranged in the uprights of the framework.

A stream of water is constantly poured on the calcareous matter through the aperture which is arranged in the tray.

In proportion as the rounding process advances, the volume of the material diminishes, and the wooden tray descends, constantly touching, though lightly, the calcareous matters, which thus obtain a round form more speedily.

When the globes are well rounded, they are again placed between two millstones, arranged in the same manner as those for rounding with the exception that the stone tray is replaced by a wooden one; the globes thus turn between two wooden trays until the polish is obtained. This process seems to merit the preference.

§ 173. To color the Marbles which are of a light and single shade, the following method is adopted:

The colors generally used are blue, red, and green; these mineral colors are reduced to a fine powder.—The globes are placed in the millstone used in polishing, upon which a few pinches of the color are thrown, several turns are then given to the millstone; after which, the color being thus evenly spread over the surface of the globes, a few pinches of sulphur, finely crushed and sifted, are thrown upon them; the millstone is then turned more rapidly, and, as the globes become heated, the sulphur burns the color, and thus gives to the globes a finer lustre. In the manufacture of Marbles of serpentine, or other hard material, a grindstone with groovings is substituted for the millstone of which we have just spoken, or, which is better, one in brass, also grooved. For this, much more water is necessary, but the same result is obtained as in the ordinary Marbles.

SECTION SECOND.

VARIOUS RECIPES.

RECIPE OF A WAX VARNISH FOR THE PRESERVATION OF STATUES AND MARBLES EXPOSED TO THE ACTION OF THE AIR.

§ 174. This varnish is obtained by melting two parts of wax, in eight parts of very pure essence of turpentine.

When the statues are removed from the *atelier* of the sculptor, this varnish should be carefully applied, heating it and spreading it so that it may not be of sufficient thickness to destroy the harmony of the figures.

This varnish may be used upon statues which have been cleansed with water dashed with hydrochloric acid, but they must be perfectly dry when the application is made.

A similar operation upon busts, statues, vases, cups, or any other ornaments in plaster, will preserve them from injury.

———

SECTION THIRD.

MOSAIC UPON MARBLE BY ABSORPTION OF COLORS.

§ 175. It is difficult to resolve the problem of the effect of the absorption of colors, both in respect to their lustre and durability, and also of the use which should be made of them. Many of the secrets of the ancients, when discovered, benefit us but little at the present time, since our tastes differ widely from theirs, as well as our fortunes, and the style of our houses.

Few of our buildings are rich enough to warrant the decoration of their pavements with the veritable mosaics; the painted mosaic seems hardly suitable to fill its place, yet this decoration may be employed in objects of less importance; and what we have already said in respect to the utility of paintings upon Marble, may be also applicable to the mosaics of which we are speaking, and which are, in truth, but a species of painting.

The art of making mosaics in Marble by the absorption of colors. was first discovered in Italy.

This process has been experimented upon by two English chemists who have obtained the following results :

1. The solution of nitrate of silver penetrates the Marble deeply, communicating to it a deep red color.

2. The solution of nitro muriate of gold does not penetrate it as deeply, but produces a very fine violet color.

3. The solution of verdigris penetrates the Marble the twelfth of an inch, giving to the surface a fine light green color.

4. The solutions of gum dragon and of gamboge also penetrate it; the first producing a fine red, and the second a yellow color.

To cause these two substances to deeply penetrate it, the Marble should be first well polished with pumice stone, after which the substances should be dissolved in warm alcohol, and applied with a small brush.

All the dyes of wood, those of Brazil, Campeachy, etc., made with alcohol, penetrate the Marble deeply.

5. The tincture of cochineal, prepared in this manner with the addition of a little alum, gives a fine scarlet color to the Marble, penetrating it one-fifth of an inch. This Marble resembles the African closely.

6. The artificial orpiment, dissolved in ammonia and laid on the Marble with a brush, produces a yellow color in a few moments, which becomes more brilliant when exposed to the air.

7. To all the other substances employed in this use, we should add white wax mixed with coloring matters; this when placed on the marble, in a melted state, soon penetrates it.

8. If the verdigris is boiled in the wax and then laid melted upon the marble with an instrument, it will be seen on its removal when cold, that the design has penetrated the surface to the depth of from one-third to half an inch; the color is a very pure green, resembling that of the emerald.

§ 176. To facilitate this work, we shall enter into a few details respecting it. Thus, when several colors are to be successively used without blending them and destroying the clearness of the design, it is necessary to proceed in the following manner.

9. The dyes obtained by spirits of wine and the oil of turpentine should be laid on the marble when it is heated, particularly in the execution of delicate designs, but the dragons' blood and gamboge may be used on the marble when cold. For this they must be dissolved in alcohol, and the gamboge used first; the solution of this gum is quite clear, but soon becomes troubled and gives a yellow precipitate, which is used to obtain a brighter color. The lines drawn by this solution are then heated by passing a plate of iron or a chafing dish filled with lighted charcoal, over the surface of the marble, at the distance of half or two-thirds of an inch from it. It is then left to cool, after which the lines which have not been penetrated by the

color are heated in the same manner. When the yellow coloring has been applied, the solution of dragons' blood, which should be concentrated as much as possible, is employed in the same manner as that of the gamboge; and while the Marble is warm, the other vegetable tints which do not require so strong a degree of heat in order to penetrate the Marble, may also be applied. The design is finally completed by the colors mixed with wax, which should be applied with the utmost care, as the slightest excess of the proper degree of heat will cause them to spread, for which reason they are less suited to delicate designs.

IMITATIONS OF MOSAICS.

§ 177. If the new mosaics are not admired, the imitations can scarcely be expected to meet with more favor.

However, they are sometimes demanded of Marble workers, and, when the price of the genuine mosaics is objected to, they endeavor to make the imitations in the best possible manner; if one can give the name of mosaic to those medleys of indiscriminate colors which have been attempted in some buildings; *L'Hotel des Finances, Rue de Rivoli*, for instance.

The desire for the production of novelties has given rise to several processes, which are announced as inven tions, but which are often only the reproduction of abortive attempts, or abandoned methods.

We do not say that the process of M. Dubreuil should be classed among these, but we give it as published by the government, without guaranteeing it.— His design is, to make imitations of mosaics, by the incorporation of colors in all kinds of calcareous stones, or gypseous matter, either smooth or sculptured. He gives the following method of proceedure:

Select calcareous or other stones; those which are fine grained and white, are best suited to mosaics, arrange these and smooth them as much as possible. These stones should be perfectly dry before the execution of the proposed designs.

The penetrating colors suited to dyeing, as well as inks (without gum,) are preferable; the artist should study these in order to prepare the tones best suited to this work. For this purpose, he can make trials upon pieces, to obtain the effects of the Marble which he wishes to produce, as well as the purity of the touch.

After the tracing of the design, you put in the colors which you deem suitable with a brush, leave them to dry, and then pour vitriol diluted with water, over the work.

With pumice and the same water, you then carefully smooth and unite the pieces, taking care to remove the mud which is formed.

The whole being washed and wiped by means of a soft stone and the same water, you polish and dry it a second time, and, in order to give it more vigor, you pass oil lightly over the colors with a brush, after which you again leave it to dry. You then obtain a fine polish by rubbing it with a dry linen cloth, which completes the operation.

To execute mosaic and other paintings upon gypseous stones and alabaster, after having selected the layer, coating, or block, which you deem suitable, you arrange your stone according to the demand, sculptured, or with a plane surface.

You then expose it to a heat sufficiently intense to calcine to the state of plaster, all the surfaces which you wish to paint and harden, to the depth of one-fifth or sixth of an inch; you then cool it, and pass a file or sand paper lightly over the surface, to cleanse any parts which may have been soiled by fire. .

You then trace the design, and put in, with the brush, the colors which have already been described, taking care to use a sufficient quantity to enable them to penetrate deeply enough.

The small pieces, which do not crack like the larger ones in hardening, may be entirely calcined.

Your design being executed, you pour alum water over the whole work, steeping the stone in it until it rejects it.

When you judge it to be entirely hardened, you wash the piece well in order to remove the refuse of the color remaining on the surface, and finish this stone in the same manner as the preceding ones, with the sole difference of using alum, in preference to the vitriolic acids.

You can give any forms you choose to the stones, whether in plane surfaces, or in reliefs, statues, vases, tables, chimney-pieces, and other articles.

§ 178. To obtain from gypseous materials, molded articles resembling Marble, after having first calcined the gypsum, reduce it to a very fine powder. The molding is executed in the following manner:

Take a mold of great solidity, and place the gypsum in it in thin layers, taking care to compress each layer in order to strengthen it.

The desired thickness being obtained, place several folds of linen or cloth upon it, moistened with common water, or with a solution of alum, which is preferable; and submit the mold in this state, to a strong, quick pressure, which instantly causes the moisture to penetrate to the bottom of the mold through the gypseous powder, thus giving it the proper consistency. The article is then taken from the mold and left to dry, after which it is set up and polished. If common water is used in the operation, the surface of the piece must be washed with a solution of alum when taken from the mold.

§ 179. In order to obtain the accidental shades which the different kinds of Marble naturally present, coloring matters (the mineral ones are better,) should be mixed with the gypseous powder. This mixture, thrown at hazard into the material which is to fill the mold, produces, by employing the methods before described, solid masses, imitating the natural Marbles.

To obtain mosaics, fill up the mold a little way with pulverized gypsum, either colored or white, then dexterously remove a portion of this coating, which has been sunk in such a manner as to leave the design to be produced upon the bottom of the mold, and is thus hollowed out; fill up these cavities with a colored gypseous powder, sunk in proportion, and finally fill the mold to the desired thickness with the gypseous powder, always compressing the layers, and proceeding as before described; a mass of great purity, bearing upon its surface the design in mosaic, is thus obtained.

If the pieces demand a greater thickness, fill up the mold with plaster tempered with pure water, place this upon the prepared materials when it begins to set, and place it under a strong pressure; this produces the same effect as the linen, and gives to the article the desired thickness by its inseparable adhesion to it.

When taken from the mold, the surface of the piece should be moistened with alum water. This method may always be employed when colored materials are to be worked.

The same results are also obtained in the execution of all kinds of relief, whether alto or basso, these may also serve, if necessary, by reason of their hardness, as molds for works of art.

All of these articles are polished with pumice and polishing stone.

Stuccos and other moist materials, when prepared, placed in a mold and covered over with dry, powdered plaster, and subjected to these operations, also acquire a great degree of hardness.

ANOTHER IMITATION OF MOSAIC.

§180. M. Simon, of Strasbourg, describes a simple method of giving to stone the appearance of Marble. Upon a stone covered with thick varnish, he says, trace the design which you wish to obtain in mosaic; pour acid upon the stone after having first surrounded the sketch with a waxen border, the lines are thus acted upon, and a greater or less depth, as may be wished, obtained; then wash it well with water, and fill the hollow lines with different colored stuccos, which soon harden; after this, polish the surface, and you have the designs in mosaic.

SECTION FOURTH.

CLEANSING OF MARBLES.

§ 181. The scraping of Marbles, which have been blackened or turned green by the air and dampness, has long been considered inexpedient, since, whatever precautions may be taken, the work which is to be restored is always scratched more or less, and it is impossible to practice it in the excavated parts without breaking the delicate sculptures, or causing sad incongruities between the designs in relief and those which are sculptured. It is therefore very desirable to find a wash that may be substituted for this destructive process. Several persons have described powders and waters, with which experiments have been made at the Luxembourg and other places, but none seem to be satisfactory. Alkalized water, prepared with potash, has also been proposed, as well as water dashed with hydrochloric acid.

In respect to soiled articles, which have not been tarnished by exposure to the open air; to restore their original color, it is sufficient to use the potash water, then to wash them in pure water, and finally, to finish them with the chlorureted water. Soap and water is often sufficient in such cases; it is spread on with a brush, and introduced into the sculptured parts by a somewhat stiff pencil.

I have heard a kind of varnish made of white wax highly extolled as a preservative; this is laid on by means of heat, and is afterwards rubbed with a cushion; it is said that this varnish was used by the ancients, and that the preservation of their *chefs d' œuvre* may be attributed to this; but proof has never been given of the efficacy of this method, which seems, like the rest, to be difficult of application.

The water and hydrochloric acid have been successfully tried in the *Place de la Concorde*, upon the statues and stone balustrades which ornament it, and the architect who superintended its use, considered it the most economical and expedient method known. The essential point in this operation is, to always use water which is perfectly clean, and in an abundant quantity. Showering by a garden pump, or a syringe with several holes, appears to me to be the best method of removing the chlorureted water from all the places in which it may rest despite the washing with the brush.

SECTION FIFTH.

OF POZZOLANA.

§ 182.   Pozzolana may be classed among the number of natural cements which are often needed by the Marble-worker, but which are rarely used on account of the difficulty of procuring them.   This is a natural cement, formed by volcanic scorias and lavas.   It was much used by the Romans for aqueducts, reservoirs, and all works exposed to a constant moisture.   Pozzolana, when mixed with the requisite proportions of good lime, sets in the water, and forms a mortar so adhesive and compactly united, that it can resist the action of the waves without suffering the least change.

There are several varieties of pozzolana, namely: First, The gravelly and compact, and the basaltic pozzolana. The compact lava and basalt, reduced to small splinters or gravelly fragments, either by nature or by pulverization in the mills used by the Dutch for crushing a softer lava, known by the name of *tras* or Andernach stone, also furnishes an excellent pozzolana, which may be used either in or out of the water.

Second. The porous pozzolana, formed by spongy lavas, which are crumbly, and reduced to powder or small irregular grains. This is the common pozzolana which abounds in the suburbs of Bayes, Pozzuoli, Naples, Rome, and in many parts of the Vivarais, etc. The ferruginous origin of these lavas having passed through different modifications, varieties in the colors of these volcanic earths have been produced; there are red, black, reddish, grey, brown, violet, and other colors. All of these, when mixed with lime, possess the property of acquiring a great solidity in water.

PUMICE STONE.

§ 183. This stone, so light, porous, and useful in almost all the arts, in Marble working most especially, is used for polishing, either in powder or in fragments; it removes the asperities, and prepares the material for receiving the last polish.

M. Daubenton was the first tb observe and remark that the pumice stones were composed of particles of an almost perfect glass, and M. Dolomieu has also made many reliable observations respecting the origin and nature of this volcanic production; he has observed in his Voyages, that the island of Lipari is the immense warehouse which furnishes pumice stones to all Europe, and that several mountains on this island are entirely composed of it; be also says that he has found isolated fragments in a white, mealy powder, which was itself but a pulverable pumice.

The substance of these stones, particularly of the lighter ones, is in a state of *frit*, closely resembling a perfect glass; their texture is fibrous, their grain rough and dry, they look shining and silky, and are much lighter than either the porous, or cellular lavas. This distinguished traveler points out four species of pumice, which differ from each other in the closeness of the grain, the weight, the texture, and the arrangement of the pores.

" The pumice stones," says he, " appear to have flowed in the same manner as the lavas, forming like them, broad currents, which have been discovered, lying at different depths above each other, around the mountains of Lipari. . . . . The heavier pumice stones occupy the lower part of the currents or masses, the lighter stones being above them; the same is also true of the lavas, the lighter and more porous always occupying the upper part."

SECTION SIXTH.

DIFFERENT DESIGNS AND CONDITIONS OF THE EXECUTION OF WORKS.

§ 184. The execution of funereal monuments, either in stone, marble, or in stone mixed with ornaments of marble, is one of the branches of this art which affords most employment to Marble workers. By visiting the various cemeteries, an idea can be formed of the diversity of the tastes, and of the intellectual or pecuniary abilities of those who erect them. One likes to fancy on seeing the expression of sorrow happily rendered, that these mourning monuments betoken less of the pride than of the sorrow of the survivors. The artists are strangers to the inscriptions which they engrave upon the marble. These being dictated by relatives and friends, they do not incur the responsibility of them; notwithstanding they have the right to give their opinion, and it would be rendering an important service to families to counsel them to make these as imple as possible. What we say respecting inscriptions will also apply to the monuments themselves When they are large and costly, they are often under the direction of an architect, and in this case, the Marble worker has only to follow the design that is given him.

When the family address themselves exclusively to the Marble worker, he makes his estimate, and when it is accepted, contracts with the mason to determine the part of each in the stipulated price, or to fix the price of the mason, who stands in the same relation to the Marble worker as he, in the preceding hypothesis, stood in respect to the architect.

As to the various forms of funereal monuments, although their general forms are similar, there are many shades of distinction which should be observed, in respect to good taste and social propriety; thus, the tomb of a woman or a young girl should not resemble that of a scholar, a warrior, a great artist, an orator, or a man of letters. There should always be some distinguishing point, though the form may be the same.

Let us take, for example, a simple form; this may be applicable to the whole world if no inscription is placed upon it. The grief which has erected it will admit no one in its confidence. The tomb will neither attract admiration or criticism from any.

But if there is an inscription, an exterior ornament should harmonize with the idea it expresses; sometimes, a lily cut off near its bloom will mutely tell of a young girl; sometimes, a wreath of falling roses will speak of a young female; sometimes, a crown of laurel will remind us of the modest and lamented warrior; sometimes, the page of a book, the image of a lyre, indicate an author, a musician, etc.

When the monument is a large one, the ornaments are of a higher order; these demand the hand of the sculptor, and should consist of emblems suited to re-call the memory of the life of the dead.

There are some tombs which only suit the pride of a rich heir. They have a sort of coquetry, which would be ridiculous on the tomb of an old man or a warrior.

Others, on the contrary, by their magisterial gravity, by sculpture, or the execution of palms, a crown, a broken sword, or some other ornament, are suited to the station in society which the man filled during his life.

We shall limit our remarks respecting the construction of costly monuments, as the direction of these works does not properly belong to Marble workers but to architects. All monuments, whether small or great, are generally modified copies of some few especial styles, and these modifications may be infinitely reproduced and varied. Besides which, the beauty of the Marbles creates more real difference than the diversity of form.

As to the price which these monuments should command, this depends entirely upon the name of the artist, the materials, and the style of the workmanship, which also includes the ornaments, which often require more time than the work itself.

There are head-stones, tombs, monuments, and family sepulchres, for two hundred dollars; they can also be purchased for twenty thousand; the time necessary for their execution differs as widely as the price.

The best method of not deceiving one's self or being deceived is, to demand an estimate, arrange a plan, and make no change in its execution without inserting a supplementary article in the contract.

Besides, the Marble workers are willing to contract at the most reasonable prices. A reasonable profit belongs to them, and the interest of the purchaser, as well as that of the Marble worker, demands that they shall have this; as to do his work well, the artist should have the hope of being compensated for his labor.

SECTION SEVENTH.

CHIMNEY-PIECE IN MALACHITE.

§ 185. Although works executed in malachite do not properly belong to the art of the Marble worker, we wish to speak of a very remarkable work of this kind.

This is a chimney-piece which is executed in what is termed the style of *Louis Quatorze*, and is truly admirable.

It is five feet in height, and more than six and a

half feet in width. The frame supports three slopings at the base of a spherical cornice in the coin; this cornice enters by the shaft and rounds towards the capital, and is terminated by a chimera supporting the upper cornice; these chimeras, as well as the fantastical figure in the centre of the mantel, are surrounded with arabesques and garlands in ormolu. Upon each side of the hearth, a Venus is half reclining upon ornaments, also in ormolu. The inside of the chimney-piece is of brass, and is also ornamented. This chimney-piece is valued at $7,500; this demonstrates sufficiently that the materials and ornaments which compose and decorate it are very costly. We shall now speak further of the malachite.

The malachite, traces of which are found in copper mines, is a mineral of irregular formation, which is only found in small masses, and is extremely rare.— It is only in Siberia that this carbonate of copper is found in blocks of greater or less size.

Prince Demidoff possesses estates in Siberia upon which large blocks have been found within a few years.

The extreme density of malachite, the fineness of its grain, and its hardness, render it susceptible of a very fine polish; the wavy reflections which show from the ground, with the shade which it presents, give it a sort of green color, full of lustre and harmony.

It is very difficult to work, and somewhat resembles those magnificent mosaics of the Vatican, which represent the admirable productions of Raphael and Michael Angelo; we do not make this comparison without design, as it explains the high price of the works composed of this material.

The museum of the mines, at St. Petersburg, contains a block weighing 317,592 pounds; this block was the most remarkable one known, previous to the discovery which was made in 1835, on the western side of the Ural Mountains, of a block weighing about 13,233 pounds. It is probably this, which has been cut to form a magnificent portal, and a vase of the greatest beauty, the value of which is estimated at nearly $82,000. These *chefs d'œuvre* excite the admiration of scholars and artists, but they will never become popular.

Malachite, in truth, can never be employed except for ornament, until some quarry easily worked shall have been discovered. But there is nothing to prevent the reproduction in fine Marble, or in porphyry, of the works which M. Demidoff has caused to be executed in malachite. It is with this view that we have described this magnificent chimney-piece, whose beautiful design is equally applicable to all other ornamental chimney-pieces.

SECTION EIGHTH.

ANCIENT AND MODERN PROCESSES FOR PAINTING OR COLORING MARBLES.

ANCIENT PROCESS FOR PAINTING ON MARBLES.

§ 186. We have already said and proved several times, that many of the *new inventions* are merely the reproductions of ancient methods, which have been abandoned for some unknown cause. We find a new proof of this in the *Dictionnaire de l'Industrie*, published in 1785, and it is somewhat remarkable that, even at that period, this invention was not given as a new one.

We make the following extract from page 408, vol. 4, of the *Encyclopedie de Diderot*, where the article may be found :

" In order to prepare a liquor which will penetrate into the interior of Marble in such a manner that one can paint on the surface, designs which seem to be within the material, it is necessary to proceed in the following manner :

" Take of aqua fortis and aqua regia, each two ounces, one ounce of salts of ammonia, two drachms of the best spirits of wine, as much gold as can be

bought for a hundred pence, and two drachms of pure
silver.   When you are furnished with these materials
and have calcined the silver, put it in a vial, and having poured upon it the two ounces of aqua fortis, leave
it to evaporate; you will thus have a water which will
at first give a blue color, and finally a black.   Calcine
the gold in the same manner, put it in the vial, and,
pouring the aqua regia upon it, leave it to evaporate.
Finally pour your spirits of wine upon the salts of
ammonia, leaving it also to evaporate; you will
thus have a golden colored water which will furnish
different colors.

"In this manner you can make many dyes of various colors, by the use of other metals.   This being
done, by the aid of the two others you can paint
whatever you may wish upon the softest kind of white
Marble, repeating the operation every day for some
time by adding new liquor to the same figures; you
will then find that the painting has penetrated the
Marble in such a manner that, in cutting it in any
manner you may please, it will always present the same
figure on both sides."

MODERN PROCESSES FOR DEEPLY COLORING MARBLES.

§ 187. We will not repeat here what we have already said several times, particularly at the head of
the preceding paragraph; yet we find it curious and
useful to compare the ancient methods with the mod-

ern ones, and we confine ourselves to the remark that the first have the advantage of experience.   We may add that if they have been abandoned, it is because this experience has demonstrated their defects, and, consequently, that new inventions must be accepted cautiously, and with reserve.   .

To succeed in the coloring of Marbles, the pieces of Marbles upon which the experiments are made should be well polished, and free from any spots or veins.   The harder the Marble, the better it supports the heat necessary to the operation; on this account alabaster and the common soft white Marble are not suitable for the purpose which we 'propose.   Heat is always necessary, to open the pores of the Marble and thus to prepare it, for the reception of colors, but it never should be heated to a red heat, as the fire then alters the contexture of the Marble, burns the colors, and destroys their beauty.

Too slight a degree of heat is as bad as one too great, for in this case, though the Marble takes the color, it does not retain it well and is not penetrated deeply enough.   There are some colors which it will even take when cold, but these never fix as well as when a proper degree of heat is employed.

The proper degree of heat is that which, without reddening the Marble, is intense enough to cause the liquor which is on its surface to boil.   The menstruums which are used to incorporate the colors, should be. varied according to the nature of the color employed; a lixivium made with the urine of the horse or dog, mixed with four parts of quick-lime and one of potash, is excellent for certain colors, the common ley of wood ashes is good for others; for some, the spirits of wine is better, some others require oily liquors, or common white wine.

The colors which succeed best with the different menstruums are the following: blue-stone dissolved in six times its quantity of spirits of wine or a urinous lixivium, and the color called litnus by the painters, dissolved in common lixivium of wood; the extract of saffron and the color made from the fruit of the buck-thorn, called sap green by the painters, both succeed very well when dissolved in urine or quick-lime, and tolerably in the spirits of wine.

Vermilion, and the fine powder of cochineal, also dissolve well in the same liquids.

Dragons' blood succeeds very well in the spirits of wine, which is also used for the dye of Campeachy wood.

The root of the alkanet gives a very fine color, but the only menstruum suited to it is turpentine, as neither the spirits of wine or any lixivium has the power to dissolve it.

There is still another kind of dragons' blood, called dragon's blood in tears, which gives a beautiful color when mixed with urine alone.

§ 188. Besides these mixtures of colors and men-

struums, certain colors can be put on dry and unmixed; such as the purest dragons' blood for the red,
the gamboge for the yellow, the green wax for a kind
of green, the common sulphur, pitch and turpentine
for a brown color.

For all these experiments, the Marble must be considerably heated, and the dry colors then rubbed upon
the block.

Some of these colors, properly applied, remain immovable, some are changed and finally effaced by
others; thus, the red color produced by dragon's
blood or the decoction of Campeachy wood, is entirely
effaced by the oil of tartar, without the polish of the
Marble receiving any injury.

A beautiful golden color is produced in the following manner: Take equal quantities of the crude salts
of ammonia, of vitriol, and of verdigris, the white
vitriol is the best for this purpose; grind these together, and reduce them all to a very fine powder.

All the shades of red and yellow may be given to
the Marble with the solutions of dragons' blood and
gamboge, by reducing these gums to powder and grinding them with spirits of wine in a glass mortar.

But, when little is required, the best method is to
mix one of these powders with spirits of wine in a silver spoon, and hold it over a heated brasier; this extracts a fine color, and, by dipping a small brush in
it, the finest veins may be made upon the cold
Marble.

When this is afterwards heated over sand from the fire, or in a baker's oven, the coloring will be absorbed and will remain perfectly distinct upon the stone.

It is very easy, by the same means, to give a ground of a red or a yellow color to Marble, leaving white veins upon it.

This is done by covering the parts designed to retain their whiteness, with white paint, or even with two or three folds of paper; either of these will prevent the penetration of the color in this part.

All the shades of red may be given to Marble simply with the aid of this gum. A weak coloring, applied without the assistance of heat, will produce a pale flesh color, but the stronger the coloring is made the deeper will the color be; to this the action of heat contributes much. By adding a little pitch to the coloring, a black shade, or all the varieties of dark red, can be given.

The archil of the Canary Islands, a species of moss, simply diluted in water and applied when cold to the Marble, communicates to it a beautiful blue color, which is more precious, as this color is rarely found in Marbles; by putting on the coloring in proportion as it dries, it becomes very fine in less than twenty-four hours, and penetrates deeply.

If the paste of archil is used, which is a preparation of the plant with lime and fermented urine, the color obtained will be more of a violet than blue; to obtain a perfect blue it must be diluted in lemon juice ; this acid will not injure the Marble, as it has been weakened by its action upon the archil.

Large blue veins may thus be formed upon the cold, white Marble, which produces a beautiful effect, but as this color is apt to spread, it will not be pure or exact unless the colored parts are instantly touched with dragons' blood or gamboge, which checks it.

It may also be checked with wax, either colored, if colored veins are required, or white, if they are to remain white.

This blue color, which penetrates the Marble more than an inch, also renders it softer ; this, however, is but a slight objection, as it is absorbed in but few places, and also possesses sufficient solidity to last many years without suffering any material change.

FIGURES IN RELIEF UPON MARBLE.

§ 189. A method has also been discovered for tracing figures in relief upon Marble with great facility. For this purpose, the desired figures are first traced upon the Marble with chalk, they are then covered with a coat of varnish, made of common Spanish sealing-wax, dissolved in spirits of wine ; after which a mixture of equal parts of acid of salts and distilled vinegar is poured upon the Marble, which corrodes the ground while the figures remain in relief, as if engraved at the cost of much time and expense.

PICTURES IN STUCCO.

§ 190. We have already described the composition and working of stucco at the present day, but we find some things more perfect in the ancient methods than in the modern.

The following extract was written in 1781.

" There is still another method of working in stucco which is superior to this, as by it pieces are so beautifully executed as to resemble the finest paintings. Landscapes are made of this stucco, and we have seen at one of the exhibitions of the Gallery, a flower picture of the greatest beauty, in which all the colors were shaded as if they had been laid on with a brush. Indeed the manner in which these pieces are executed may be regarded as a species of painting in stucco, as may be seen from the process.

" The stucco, or artificial Marble, of which these beautiful works are made, is a composition of which plaster forms the entire base ; the hardness that may be given it, the different colors with which it may be mixed, and the polish of which it is susceptible, renders it suitable to imitate, with almost perfect exactness, the most costly Marbles.

COLORING OF ARTIFICIAL MARBLES.

§ 191. This coloring, which is now given us as a novelty, was clearly described in some very ancient works, which were copied by the authors of the Ency-clopedia, published in 1780, in the following words:

" When any Marble is to be imitated, soak the colors which are found in this Marble in warm glue water, in different small pots; temper a little plaster with each of these colors, then make a cake of each color, a little larger than the hand, place all these cakes alternately upon each other, placing those of the prevailing color in the greatest number, or thicker.

" Then turn these cakes, thus flatly arranged, upon the side; cut them and place them quickly upon the core of the work, afterwards flattening them down.

" By this means, the fantastical design of the dif-ferent colors of the Marble can be perfectly repre-sented.

" If the Marbles termed Breccias are to be imitated, mix in the composition of these cakes, when spread upon the core, different sized pieces of the plaster tempered with the color of the Breccia; these pieces, when flattened down, form very good imitations of Breccias.

" It should be observed that in all these operations, the glue water should be warm, without which the plaster will set too quickly, without giving time to work it."

SECTION NINTH.

TURNED MARBLE.

ORNAMENTAL CLOCKS, CUPS, CANDLESTICKS.

§ 192. Cylindrical articles, such as columns of clocks, chimney-pieces, cups, vases, candlesticks, basins, etc., are made in the lathe by professional workmen; and even those vases resting upon square or octagonal pedestals, may also be worked by the turner. This is also true of the torso columns of temples and churches.

The turning-lathe is far more expeditious and surer than the chisel; it must be an extraordinary event to cause the failure of an article in the turner's hand; but this is not. the case when it is worked with the mallet and chisel.

There are many articles which cannot be executed with the chisel, such as delicate parts of some clocks, candelabras, and candlesticks which are partly in Marble and partly in bronze.

All the fine Marbles unite perfectly with green or gilded bronze. This is true respecting the pedestals of clocks, and the stems, more or less ornamented, which support vases and cups.

It is not an uncommon thing to see workmen understanding the art of the Marble worker, eagerly desire

to be able to turn the articles which they apply as or.
naments to works which they execute in the *atelier*.

This is expensive, owing to the room and the tools
required ; yet it would be very convenient, especially
in the provinces, where it is not easy to find turners
capable of making the vases, urns, columns, and rose-
work which are needed.

These workmen would have many advantages over
the ordinary turners, as they would understand the
nature of Marble, the mode of polishing, and the manner of cementing the defective parts.

It would be an excellent plan for a Marble yard to
have a turning-lathe for the use of those workmen who
have a taste for the art of the turner.

VOCABULARY

A.

ALABASTER.—A species of white Marble, very transparent, and easily worked, which is especiallv used for clocks and mantel vases. There are several varieties of colored alabaster, besides a kind called agate, which is greenish, mixed with a clear bister.

ANTIQUE MARBLE.—The beautiful white Marble taken from the ancient quarries of Greece, specimens of which still exist in superb statues and magnificent bas-ruliefs.

ALKANET.—A plant, a species of anchusa, the root of which affords a reddish purple dye.

ARCHIL.—A lichen, which grows on rocks in the Canary and Cape de Verd Islands, and which yields a rich purple color. It is bruised between stones, and moistened with strong spirits of wine mixed with quick-lime.— It first takes a purplish red color, and then turns to blue. In the first state it is called *archil*, in the second, *litmus*.

ARRIS.—Edges formed by the meeting of two surfaces; applied particularly to the edges of mouldings, and the raised edges which separate the flutings in a Doric column.

B.

BLEU TURQUIN.—Marble taken from the coasts of Genoa and several other quarries. It is of a deep blue upon a white ground, mixed with grey spots and large veins.

BLOCK OF MARBLE.—A piece, rough from the quarry.

BRECCIA—A species of Marble composed of a mass of small pebbles, closely cemented together in such a manner that, when broken, they form *brèches*, or notches; whence its name.

BROCATELLE.—A Marble of which the color is a mixture of grey, yellow, red, and dove shades. It is very costly, and is scarcely ever used except for ornaments.

BURIN.—A steel blade, nearly square, and often squared and sharpened at one end in the form of a grain of barley.

BOASTING TOOL.—A kind of chisel with a handle, used by sculptors who work in stucco and plaster, to boast their works.

BOASTED MARBLE.—That which is worked with the double etching needle, or chisel. The best are made of cast steel.

C.

CHEVAL DE TERRE.—The spaces filled with clay which are sometimes discovered in the blocks of Marble, and which would spoil the finest works. These accidents tend to increase the price of Marble working. as they may result in great injury to the Marble worker

CEMENT.—This is both natural and artificial; the first is that which acts in the formation of the Marble, joining together the different parts; the second is composed by the Marble workers for uniting and gluing the Marbles when worked, and for filling the cavities which are found in some stones and Marbles.

CHISEL IN MARTELINE.—A tool of the Marble worker; it is steeled on one end and furnished with small points to shell off and boast the Marble.

CHISELS.—Small steel tools which are used to aid the sledge hammer or mallet in working Marble or stone.— Every Marble worker has a collection of them. The finest are of cast steel.

COMPARTMENT OF MARBLE PAVEMENTS.—The symmetrical arrangement of blocks or tiles of different colored Marbles, or of Marbles and lias stone.

COMPASS.—A hinged tool with two pointed branches, used in all the arts and trades for measuring lines, and tracing discs, ovals and circles of all kinds upon wood, minerals or metals. There is a kind with a hinge and pencil case in one of its branches, but this is not generally used by Marble workers.

COMPASS OF THE FIGURE EIGHT.—This is to measure on one side, giving the measure on the other; it is principally used in the turning lathe.

COMPASS OF DEPTH.—This compass is designed to find the depth of a diameter. The branches are bent, so that the article to be measured can pass between them. The best have the arc of a circle fixed at one branch and passing through the other, under a thumb screw which fastens them open as long as may be wished.

CALLOSITIES OF MARBLE.—These defects are to Marble what knots are to wood.

CRUMBLY MARBLE.—That which, when worked, does not retain its sharp arris, but crumbles and falls off.

D.

DOG'S TOOTH. A kind of puncheon used by Marble workers.

DRILL. A pointed instrument, used for boring holes.

E.

EMERY DUST. A species of powdered corundrum, taken from under the wheels upon which lapidaries polish stones. It is used by the Marble workers for polishing Marble.

F.

FELD SPAR. A vitreous substance, which is one of the essential constituents of granite, mica, and porphyry, and enters into the constitution of nearly all the volcanic rocks.

FRAISE. A tool used to enlarge the holes which are made in the Marble with a drill or common auger. It is of a slightly conical form, and is grooved roughly to aid its effect upon the Marble.

G.

GRADINE. A kind of puncheon used by the Marble worker.

GRANITE. A very hard Marble, marked with small, condensed spots. The most common colors are grey, greyish white, and flesh red; some are green, violet, etc.

GYPSUM. A calcareous matter, impregnated with too great a quantity of vitriolic acid to permit it to be affected by any other acid.

H.

HOUGUETTE. An etching needle, flat and steeled.

HOOKED TOOL.—A kind of sharp chisel which is wholly of steel, or of iron steeled on one end, which is half bent in a hooked shape; this chisel is used where the square chisel cannot penetrate and where the etching needle would not be sufficient.

HEARTHS.—Pieces of Marble, from three to five feet in length, and from twenty to twenty-three inches in width, which are placed before chimney-pieces for ornament, and to preserve floorings and carpets from accidents from fire. They are both simple and composite. The simple ones are formed of a single piece without ornaments; the composite are those composed of several pieces of different Marbles, thus resembling a sort of mosaic.

J.

JASPER.—Marble of a greenish color, mixed with small red spots. There is an antique jasper with small spots of black and white.

A variety of quartz, penetrated with metallic particles.

JASPER MARBLE.—A Marble resembling the antique jasper.

L.

LAPIS.—An antique Marble of a deep blue, spotted with a deeper blue, and intermixed with a few veins of gold.— It is one of the richest, but is very rare.

LIXIVIUM.—Lye; chemical solutions; extracts and washes.

M.

MALLET.—Wooden hammers, used for beating or driving other tools employed in Marble working. The best have knobs of boxwood, alder, or horn beam. Those of iron are called sledge-hammers.

MARBLE.—A hard, calcareous stone, somewhat transparent, black or white, or veined and spotted with different colors.

MARBLE: ARTIFICIAL.—A composition of gypsum, mixed with various colors in imitation of Marble. This composition is hard and susceptible of polish, but is apt to scale off.

MARBLE PAINTING.—Painting which imitates the different colors, veins, and peculiarities of Marbles.

MARBLE WORKING.—This not only comprises the use of Marble, but also the art of sawing, cutting, and polishing it, and of restoring and repolishing it when it is old.

MARBLE WORKER.—A workman who hews, cuts, and polishes Marble.

MARTIN.—A tool which is very essential to all *ateliers*. It is a brass plate glued to a stone, with a handle attached to facilitate its movement. An aperture of an inch and a half or two inches is made in the centre of this plate and its lining, through which sand and water is passed upon the Marble to polish it. There are several sizes, some of which may be worked by an apprentice, while some require one or two workmen, according to the size of the piece to be polished and the weight of the martin.

MASTIC.—A composition of oil and different gummy substances. It is used to fill up the cavities in Marble, and to cement the pieces together after having been worked. There are mastics, also, especially for stone.

MICA.—A mineral of the same nature as quartz and jasper, and capable of being cleaved into exceedingly thin plates; one of the primitive glasses.

MADREPORE.—A species of coral of the class of Zoophytes. The species usually branch like trees or shrubs. The surface is covered with small prominences, each containing a cell.

MENSTRUUM.—A solvent; any fluid or subtilized substance which dissolves a solid body.

O.

ORMOLU.—Brass, which by a chemical process is made to assume the appearance of being gilt.

P.

PALETTE OR CONSCIENCE.—A kind of drill plate, composed of an iron plate perforated with several holes, in which the head of the drill is placed, and which is rested 'upon the breast of the workman to augment its force and diminish his labor. Drills fastened in a rod which is mounted upon a flattened knob, are sometimes substituted for this.

PAROS MARBLE.—An antique Marble which was quarried from an island of the Archipelago. It is white with a yellowish tint, and transparent.

PAPER STONE.—A round, oval, or square piece of Marble, to which a knob of Marble is attached; used to keep paper in its place upon the desk. These are made from the cuttings of slabs and other articles of Marble.

PUMICE STONE.—A substance which is frequently ejected from volcanoes; supposed to be produced by the disengagement of gas, in which the lava is in a plastic state.— It is used for polishing Marbles, either powdered or in pieces.

PLASTER STONE.—A calcareous substance, which is calcined, pulverized, and tempered with cold water to form coats of impression, and even stuccos.

PUNCHEON.—One of the tools of the Marble worker; an iron instrument, with a sharp, steeled point.

POLISHED MARBLE.—That which has been rubbed and glossed with a linen cushion, or with emery dust or pewter. There are two kinds of polish; the common, which is given to simple articles; the lustrous, which is given to articles requiring more pains, such as costly chimney-pieces, Marble furniture, clocks, .candelabras, bas reliefs, hearths, vases, and other articles of the same nature.

PORPHYRY.—The hardest of the antique Marbles, and the finest, after the Lapis. There are red, green, and grey porphyries.

PEWTER.—The ashes which results from the calcination of tin. It is much used in the arts, and also by Marble workers in polishing their works.

PUDDING-STONES.—All stones which are composed of fragments of other stones, united by a natural cement.—The Breccias are pudding-stones; yet all pudding-stones are not Breccias, as some of them are not composed of calcareous matter.

POZZOLANA.—Natural cement produced from the scoride of volcanic substances.

Q.

QUARTZ.—The first of the glasses; the essential constituent of granite and porphyry.

R.

RABAT.—Marble workers give this name to the potter s

clay which has failed in baking, and which they use to smooth down the roughness of the Marble.

RABOT.—A piece of hard wood, used in rubbing the Marble, and preparing it to receive the polish.

RASP.—A species of file, upon which the cutting prominences are distinct, being raised by punching with a point, instead of cutting with a chisel. They are flat, half rounded, and round.

ROUGH HEWN MARBLE.—That which is cut up with the saw, or squared with the mallet.

ROUND NOSED CHISEL.—A tool used by the Marble worker for sinking the Marble, and leveling the cavities.

ROUND FILE.—A kind of file, or round and pointed rasp, used by Marble workers.

ROUGH MARBLE.—That which is yet in the block.

S.

SAW, OF THE MARBLE WORKER.—It is without teeth; with a different frame from common saws, and proportioned to the pieces to be cut up. The blade of this saw is large, and strong enough to saw the Marble slowly, with the aid of sand and water which the sawer pours into the cleft. There are also two kinds of hand saws, one of which is notched, and the other smooth.

SCRAPER.—A toothed and steeled instrument, designed for sinking flutings; also a tool used by stucco workers.

SHAVE GRASS.—A kind of rough aquatic plant, sometimes called Dutch rush, or scouring rush.

SEBILLA.—A wooden bowl, designed to hold the sand and water used in sawing the Marble.

SERPENTINE.—A calcareous stone or very hard Marble, which takes a very fine polish; it derives its name from the resemblance of its grains to the spots upon the skin of a serpent.

SIMPLE COMPARTMENT.—The plan of a pavement, composed of tiles of black and white Marble, or two other colors, arranged in squares or lozenges.

SPAR.—An earthy mineral that breaks with regular surfaces, and has some degree of lustre ; a crystallized earthy mineral of a shining lustre.

STUCCO.—·An artificial stone, with which all kinds of Marbles may be imitated. In England this style of building is very common, and many brick edifices are found covered with it, sometimes in a highly ornamental manner. In the United States it has been little used.

T.

TALC.—A kind of soft, unctuous stone ; one of the constituents of Marble.

TERRASES.—Defects in Marble which are remedied by filling them with Marble powder mixed with mastic of the same color ; first cleaning out the hole, filled with a foreign substance which is neither clay, Marble or granite.

TREPAN.—A tool used for boring and drilling Marbles and hard stones. It is rarely used since the invention of the wimble, which is much better suited to the purposes for which it was used.

W.

WIMBLE.—An instrument for boring holes, turned by a handle.

Z.

ZINC.—A metal brilliantly white, with a shade of blue, which is used, either in powder or in pieces, for polishing Marbles, most especially toy Marbles.

APPENDIX

AMERICAN MARBLES.

To make this Manual complete for the use of American Marble-workers, it only remains for us to give some account of the Marbles of the United States.

Our country is rich in Marbles, but it is only in the older States that quarries have been opened or worked to any great extent. The few explorations that have been made, however, leave no doubt that inexhaustible stores of the finest qualities are packed away within the mountains and in ledges that are easily accessible. The wise policy of most of our States has caused early geological surveys to be made, and it is through their medium that the discovery of new varieties and abundant supplies will doubtless be made quite as fast as there is a demand for them.

But while none doubt the plentiful quantity of our native Marbles, there has been much skepticism as to their quality. We sent no specimens, good or bad, to the Great London Exhibition, and the world has been obliged to judge of our resources in this respect entirely by our buildings. Any bad impression that has gone forth is due not so much to the bad quality of the material itself, as to the neglect of care on the part of builders and of those entrusted with the duty of selecting Marble for our public edifices. The extraordinary representations of interested parties have foisted many miserable specimens into use. The haste of contractors has put into buildings a good many very unworthy blocks from quarries that easily might have furnished plenty of unexceptionable ones. The elementary principle very often has been neglected—that regard should be had in laying up stones, that are to bear much pressure, to the original bedding of the stone. Hence blocks which, if placed differently, would have lasted for centuries, already, after standing at right angles to their natural position but a few years, are scaling off and crumbling on their surfaces. Then it would seem as if some who have chosen the materials for our marble fronts were color-blind. Certainly nothing can look more slovenly than some patchwork fronts we are obliged to endure the sight of—first a snowy white block, next a bluish one, then one of a creamy yellow, and then one so full of fissures that the dirt lodged in it gives an appearance of some very undesirable veined variety. A slight knowledge of the geological habits of Marble would have saved many public blunders and prevented many costly mistakes. The limestone ledges which rise in smooth bleached perpendicular walls, that give no hold to lichens, and are not discolored by the solution of any of their component parts, must furnish the Marbles that will bear the weather well. While those into which rivers have cut deep channels, or which standing inland bear deep seams across their face, or which have to be dug from under the original surface of the earth, and over which much soil has accumulated, give in their very position the strongest evidence that they cannot long endure.

As we have said, few of the States or territories have been thoroughly or even casually surveyed with reference to their wealth in building materials. Yet new as our country is, and busy as our geologists have been in indicating the enterprizes which would more immediately reward industry and capital, we have already a long list of localities prolific in available Marbles. .

Maine abounds as no other State does in limestones. Some from the vicinity of Thomaston admit a fine polish. They are the blue, the clouded, the veined, and an elegant white dolomite for monuments. About Union and Machias some breccias are obtained.

Vermont is *the* Marble State, and this material will prove one of its most fruitful sources of wealth. Fine white Marble, which can be obtained in large cakes, is found along the base of the Green Mountains, for fifty miles above and below Rutland. At West Rutland statuary Marble is quarried that is surpassed by none in the world. Our own sculptors have availed themselves of it to some extent, and some orders for it from Italian sculptors at Rome have been filled. It is said to be of a finer grain, to work more easily than the foreign, and not to crumble so badly under the chisel. At this same locality is a spotted grey Marble, much used for mantels. A beautiful dark-colored article is got at Pittsford. From Shoreham and other points along Lake Champlain, black Marble is obtained. At our New York Crystal Palace Exhibition a shell Marble from Vermont, with bright red spots, attracted much attention—but it has not been worked. A serpentine recently discovered in Roxbury promises to replace the exhausted quarries of Europe. It very closely resembles the European verd antique, but where the latter has carbonate of lime, the former has carbonate of magnesia. According to Dr. Jackson, ours has a superior out-of-door durability, and longer resists decomposition from the atmosphere, from fire, and from acids. It offers no hold to moss. It cuts hard, but is sawn more easily. When polished it is of a rich and beautiful green, veined with white and mottled. The quarries of this one State produce over a million dollars annually.

Massachusetts abounds in limestones, free enough from fissure, and compact enough to admit a medium polish. Berkshire County is especially rich in such—so much so indeed that scarcely an effort has been made to obtain them elsewhere in the State. It was hoped that the bed in Stoneham, (Middlesex County,) would furnish even the rare variety used in statuary, and small specimens of it compare favorably with the

Carrara. But it is so full of fissures that blocks can seldom be obtained. The best Berkshires are of a suowy white, free from magnesia, and for a primary Marble are elegant. Occasionally, however, they are clouded and frequently are grey. The North Adams Marble is white and pure, but a little too crystaline. That of New Ashford is of a finer grain. The New York City Hall was built of the West Stockbridge Marble, and a part of the Boston State House is from the same locality. From Sheffield came the Girard College pillars. The Lee Marble is just now most prominently before the public—it being the material employed in building the extension of the Capitol at Washington. At Great Barrington is a beautiful clouded Marble, well adapted for mantels and jambs, but owing to its 40 per cent. of magnesia, is very liable to break. Prof. Hitchcock finds in this vicinity a *flexible* Marble—which, if properly wet, bends like a lath—a singular property, but not quite unknown abroad; as several tables of elastic Marble were preserved and exhibited in the house of Prince Borghese, of Rome, as great curiosities. There is a beautiful serpentine found at Lynnfield, but it is too soft. Beds of steatite, hardened by quartz or serpentine, are common too in Massachusetts. Several houses with steatite fronts have lately been erected in New York and Brooklyn—all which were furnished, however, from Middlefield, Vt. This hardened steatite will very possibly come into common use hereafter.

Rhode Island has some Marbles, but the quarries are little worked.

Connecticut forty years ago furnished the rarest and most beautiful of verd antiques. For in-door work it was admirably fitted; but exposed, as for grave-stones and monuments, it soon parted with its polish and grew dull. Though inexhaustible, the increasing expense of working it has caused it to be neglected.

Of the abundance of Marble in New York, some idea may be gained when it is stated that the State geologists announce it as present in twenty-five counties of the State. Most of the white variety is like that of Massachusetts—too highly granular and too slightly coherent to sustain heavy pressure or to endure our variable climate.

In *Clinton* County, near Plattsburg, a jet black Marble is found. *Columbia* County produces a Dolomite, which is much esteemed. Prof. HITCHCOCK thinks that if worked it might yield as fair results as the beds of Egremont. Near Hudson, in Becraft's Mountain, a beautiful grey with a tint of red is found, which resembles the Peak of Derbyshire Marble. It has been worked a little.

Dutchess produces a fine white like the Lee; and also a clouded Marble which is reported durable. *Essex* has a verd antique—a limestone through which green serpentine is diffused. *Franklin* County abounds in the white primitive. *Jefferson* and *St. Lawrence*, though very little explored, show some. In *Lewis* a dark serpentine, valuable for ornamental purposes, is found. The *New York* (Kingsbridge) limestone crumbles too easily for building purposes. *Niagara* has, near Lockport, a variegated, reddish-brown Marble, which is full of organic remains, and is of great beauty. It has been used somewhat for interiors — *Oneida* has the Trenton limestone, which finishes black and also some greys. *Onondaga* has a grey crinoidal limestone, which affords a Marble scarcely excelled by any of the sort in the country for durability, beauty, and the fineness of its polish. None of the several localities found in *Orange* County are worked. *Putnam* has both white and colored Marbles, and a serpentine that takes a good polish. Of the black Marble, rare in Europe, yet of which some old Spanish palaces were built, MATHER says there is enough sound and free from cracks in *Clinton* County to supply the world. *Rockland* has a dove-colored and a verd antique that takes a high polish. *Ulster* has, in the vicinity of Rondout and Kingston, several beds of a limestone which is susceptible of a high polish, that will some day turn out valuable black and dark-colored Marbles. But the black Marbles of Glen Falls, *Warren* County, extensively in use for mantels, take an unrivalled polish. Though the supply is inexhaustible, this article grows more and more costly in the market, owing to the increased difficulty of getting it out. There are, however, two hundred and seventy-five saws now running in the mills of that village. *Warren* County possesses, too, some verd antique, some fine grey Marble, and some veined like the Egyptian; except that the veins are white and grey where the Egyptian is yellow. It is, perhaps, more difficult to work than the imported. *Washington* County has a good clouded article. *Westchester* abounds in the Dolomite. Fair specimens may be seen in the New York Custom House, the Brooklyn Exchange, the front of Stewart's store, of the St. Nicholas Hotel, and of the store on the southwest corner of Broadway and Warren streets in New York. Marbles of inferior importance are found (grey) in *Albany*, (black) in *Schoharie*, and in *Otsego, Saratoga, Seneca*, and *Wayne*.

Pennsylvania has many quarries. The Marble so much used in Philadelphia is from Chester County.

Maryland produces a white from her "Alum Limestone;" and at the foot of the Blue Ridge and on the Potomac banks a beautiful pudding-stone polished specimens of which may be found in the pillars of the House of Representatives at Washington. The colors are very striking.

There is a good deal of Marble in *Virginia*, but it has been little quarried.

Marble is found in Laurens and Spartanburg Districts of *South Carolina*.

Some quarries have been worked in Cherokee Co., *Georgia*.

Beautiful varieties exist in *Alabama*, near the heads of the rivers, and particularly on the Cahawba and in Talladega County. Some of these are buff-colored and filled with organic remains; some are white and crystalline, and some black. In Coosa County fine statuary Marble is said to be found. From this locality most of the tombstones and furniture Marble used in the Southern part of the State are brought.

In *Ohio*, *Indiana*, and *Illinois* little pains have yet been taken to develope the mineral building materials.

Kentucky produces an inferior Marble, which, though susceptible of a high polish, is too brittle for heavy use.

Tennessee contains several beautiful varieties. A variegated one found near Nashville, lately brought to light, is likely to come into the New York market.

Wisconsin, in its northern part, has Marbles whose prevailing color is light pink, traversed by veins of deep red. It has others of blue and dove color handsomely veined; but none of them are worked to any great extent.

Veined and crystalline Marbles are found in *Missouri*. *Arkansas* is well supplied. *Iowa* is not destitute of the less valuable variety. Marble has been found in Marin County, and in some other parts of *California*. In several States which we have not named the native Marbles have been employed for building purposes, for tombstones, &c.; but in our list we have embraced the more important localities and the varieties best known.

But notwithstanding the abundance of our home supply, very much of that used for interior ornamentation is imported. According to the Report of Secretary GUTHRIE, the value of the unmanufactured Marble of foreign production imported to this country during the year ending June, 1855, was $232,385.— From this item we have only to deduct $944, the value of the foreign unmanufactured Marble exported by us during the same time, to discover just how great was our consumption of the foreign Marbles. How much of our own Marble has gone abroad we cannot say—the item not having been separately reported.

This large importation of the article may be owing to three causes. For some purposes the foreign may be a better article, or if not better, it is better known. Then there is still some prejudice, perhaps, in favor of an *imported* material, on the part of the uninformed, to which dealers must cater. But there is a stronger reason than all in the fact that the lower rates of wages abroad enable the imported article to be furnished far cheaper than that of equal excellence which lies at our very doors. Thus when the Italian statuary Marble was selling in New York at $2.50 to $3.00 per cubic foot, that from Rutland, Vt., cost $4.50.— It is, more than anything else, a question of expense, whether foreign or domestic Marbles shall be used.— We get none finer abroad than we have at home. We

have no need to send to Carrara for the capitals to
our columns, nor to Ireland for black Marble, if we
can afford to buy the best. And when capital and
the inventive arts are more directed to the business
of getting out and manufacturing Marble, it will
doubtless seem as simple to send abroad for it as it
would to imitate our fathers, and bring tomb-stones
ready made from Wales, and brick from Holland.

Our variable climate is very hard upon *poor* Marbles. Our hard rains and severe frosts are sure to
search out their fissures and flaws, and from them begin their slow work of disintegration. Many Marbles,
indeed, when properly polished, will answer for slabs
to face or veneer brick houses with, which in the block
would not answer at all.

In a late number of SILLIMAN's *Journal*, WALTER
R. JOHNSON, Esq., details some suggestive- observations upon the ability of different building materials
to endure pressure, founded on experiments that have
been recorded. Noticing that the Washington Monument at Baltimore, which was begun only in 1815,
already exhibited fractures across whole blocks in it,
he directs his special attention to the " Alum Limestone" of which it is built, and which is nearly allied
to the Sing Sing Marble of which Grace Church in
New York City is constructed. In conclusion, for
purposes of comparison, he arranges the materials
experimented on in the order of their relative value,
as determined by their power to resist crushing—

The " Alum Limestone" standing at   100
  "   Stockbridge Marble stood at   96
  "   Italian   "   "   135
  "   East Chester (N. Y.) "   171
  "   White Statuary   "   199

" Its true position," he says, "in the scale of strength among building stones, as proved both by Dr. PAGE and Mr. WYATT, is among the sandstones, not among granites, marbles, or compact limestones." Yet this is the material out of which the Washington National Monument is building, and of it, or of a still feebler Marble, as marked in the table, very many edifices have been erected, which their authors and architects flattered themselves were their enduring monuments.

When (in 1824) the American Museum was to be erected, in New York, so great was the prejudice against Marble, as a building material, that it was necessary to pardon a man at Sing Sing prison to get the contract closed. Now—and the fact shows how it has grown into popular favor—there are on Broadway, between the Bowling Green and Union Square, twenty-six Marble fronts ; in Liberty Street, sixteen ; in Cortlandt, Wall and Dey Streets, each five ; in Maiden Lane, six ; in Fulton, Vesey and Murray Streets, each seven ; in Barclay Street, eight ; in Chambers Street, ten ; and in Warren Street, eighteen, besides as many others in many other streets throughout the city.

The last census (of 1850) does not distinguish

tween the Marble and the Stone Cutters; still it may aid somewhat in getting an idea of the extent to which Marble is wrought, if we annex the following table.

NUMBER OF STONE AND MARBLE CUTTERS IN THE
UNITED STATES IN 1850.

Maine,.............	522
New Hampshire....	865
Vermont,......	265
Massachusetts,.... ....:.	2,320
Rhode Island,....	297
Connecticut,....	514
New York....:	8,443
New Jersey,....	219
Pennsylvania,..	2,114
Delaware,...... .... ,....	9
Maryland,....	381
District of Columbia,....	128
Virginia,....	427
North Carolina,.... ....- ..-- ....-	82
South Carolina,....	75
Georgia,..................	50
Florida,....	12
Alabama,.....	52
Mississippi,.....	4
Louisiana,.....	71
Texas,............................... ./...... ..	4
Arkansas,:..... ..:....	24
Tennessee,.........................	151
Kentucky,.....	226
Ohio,.....	1,453
Michigan,...:	64
Indiana,....................	248

Illinois,....   204
Missouri,.....   270
Iowa,......   69
Wisconsin,...   84
California,.....   2

TERRITORIES.

New Orleans,....   1
Oregon,....   2
Utah,...   24
                                                        ———
              Total,.. 14,076

Practical and Scientific Books,

HENRY CAREY BAIRD,

INDUSTRIAL PUBLISHER,

No. 406 Walnut Street,

PHILADELPHIA.

☞ Any of the following Books will be sent by mail, free of postage, at the publication price. Catalogues furnished on application.

American Miller and Millwright's Assistant:

A new and thoroughly revised Edition, with additional Engravings. By WILLIAM CARTER HUGHES. In one volume, 12 mo.,..$1.25

Armengaud, Amoroux, and Johnson.

THE PRACTICAL DRAUGHTSMAN'S BOOK OF INDUSTRIAL DESIGN, and Machinist's and Engineer's Drawing Companion; forming a complete course of Mechanical Engineering and Architectural Drawing. From the French of M. Armengaud the elder, Prof. of Design in the Conservatoire of Arts and Industry, Paris, and MM. Armengaud the younger, and Amouroux, Civil Engineers. Re-written and arranged, with additional matter and plates, selections from and examples of the most useful and generally employed mechanism of the day. By William Johnson, Assoc. Inst. C. E., Editor of "The Practical Mechanic's Journal." Illustrated by fifty folio steel plates and fifty wood-cuts. A new edition, 4to.,...$10.00

Among the contents are :—*Linear Drawing, Definitions and Problems*, Plate I. Applications, Designs for inlaid Pavements, Ceilings and Balconies, Plate II. Sweeps, Sections and Mouldings, Plate III. Elementary Gothic Forms and Rosettes, Plate IV. Ovals, Ellipses,

' Notice of the Important Inventions, Tariffs, and the Results of each Decennial Census. By J. Leander Bishop, M. D,: to which is added Notes on the Principal Manufacturing Centres and Remarkable Manufactories. By Edward Young and Edwin T. Freedley. In two vols., 8vo. $6.00

Bookbinding: A Manual of the Art of Book binding,

Containing full instructions in the different branches of Forwarding, Gilding and Finishing. Also, the Art of Marbling Book-edges and Paper. By James B. Nicholson. Illustrated. 12mo., cloth, ...$2.25

CONTENTS.—Sketch of the Progress of Bookbinding, Sheet-work, Forwarding the Edges, Marbling, Gilding the Edges, Covering, Half Binding, Blank Binding, Boarding, Cloth-work, Ornamental Art, Finishing, Taste and Design, Styles, Gilding, Illuminated Binding, Blind Tooling, Antique, Coloring, Marbling, Uniform Colors, Gold Marbling, Landscapes, etc., Inlaid Ornaments, Harmony of Colors, Pasting Down, etc., Stamp or Press-work, Restoring the Bindings of Old Books, Supplying imperfections in Old Books, Hints to Book Collectors, Technical Lessons.

Booth and Morfit. The Encyclopedia of Chemistry, Practical and Theoretical:

Embracing its application to the Arts, Metallurgy, Mineralogy, Geology, Medicine, and Pharmacy, By James C. Booth, Melter and Refiner in the United States Mint; Professor of Applied Chemistry in the Franklin Institute, etc.; assisted by Campbell Morfit, author of "Chemical Manipulations," etc. 7th Edition. Complete in one volume, royal octavo, 978 pages, with numerous wood cuts and other illustrations, ...:$5.00

From the very large number of articles in this volume, it is entirely impossible to give a list of the Contents, but attention may be called to some among the more elaborate, such as Affinity, Alcoholometry, Ammonium, Analysis, Antimony, Arsenic, Blowpipes, Cyanogen, Distillation, Electricity, Ethyl, Fermentation, Iron, Lead and Water.

Brewer; (The Complete Practical.)

Or Plain, Concise, and Accurate Instructions in the Art of Brewing Beer, Ale, Porter, etc., etc., and the Process of Making all the Small Beers. By M. Lafayette Byrn, M. D. With Illustrations. 12mo........ ....$1.25

Many an old brewer will find in this book valuable hints and sug-

Builder's Pocket Companion:

Containing the Elements of Building, Surveying, and Architecture; with Practical Rules and Instructions connected with the subject. By A. C. SMEATON, Civil Engineer, etc. In one volume, 12mo., ...$1.25

CONTENTS.—The Builder, Carpenter, Joiner, Mason, Plasterer, Plumber, Painter, Smith, Practical Geometry, Surveyor, Cohesive Strength of Bodies, Architect.

"It gives, in a small space, the most thorough directions to the builder, from the laying of a brick, or the felling of a tree, up to the most elaborate production of ornamental architecture. It is scientific, without being obscure and unintelligible; and every house-carpenter, master, journeyman, or apprentice, should have a copy at hand always."—*Evening Bulletin.*

Byrne. The Handbook for the Artisan, Mechanic, and Engineer,

Containing Instructions in Grinding and Sharpening of Cutting Tools, Figuration of Materials by Abrasion, Lapidary Work, Gem and Glass Engraving, Varnishing and Lackering, Abrasive Processes, etc., etc. By Oliver Byrne. Illustrated with 11 large plates and 185 cuts. 8vo., cloth,..$5.00

CONTENTS.—Grinding Cutting Tools on the Ordinary Grindstone; Sharpening Cutting Tools on the Oilstone; Setting Razors; Sharpening Cutting Tools with Artificial Grinders; Production of Plane Surfaces by Abrasion; Production of Cylindrical Surfaces by Abrasion; Production of Conical Surfaces by Abrasion; Production of Spherical Surfaces by Abrasion; Glass Cutting; Lapidary Work; Setting, Cutting, and Polishing Flat and Rounded Works; Cutting Faucets; Lapidary Apparatus for Amateurs; Gem and Glass Engraving; Seal and Gem Engraving; Cameo Cutting; Glass Engraving, Varnishing, and Lackering; General Remarks upon Abrasive Processes; Dictionary of Apparatus; Materials and Processes for Grinding and Polishing commonly employed in the Mechanical and Useful Arts.

Byrne. The Practical Metal-worker's Assistant,

For Tin-plate Workers, Braziers, Coppersmiths, Zinc-plate Ornrmenters and Workers, Wire Workers, Whitesmiths, Blacksmiths, Bell Hangers, Jewellers, Silver and Gold Smiths, Electrotypers, and all other Workers in Alloys and Metals. Edited by OLIVER BYRNE. Complete in one volume, octavo,...$7.00

It treats of Casting, Founding, and Forging; of Tongs and other Tools; Degrees of Heat and Management of Fires; Welding of

Heading and Swage Tools; of Punches and Anvils; of Hardening and Tempering; of Malleable Iron Castings, Case Hardening, Wrought and Cast Iron; the Management and Manipulation of Metals and Alloys, Melting and Mixing; the Management of Furnaces, Casting and Founding with Metallic Moulds, Joining and Working Sheet Metal; Peculiarities of the different Tools employed; Processes dependent on the ductility of Metals; Wire Drawing, Drawing Metal Tubes, Soldering; The use of the Blowpipe, and every other known Metal Worker's Tool.

Byrne. The Practical Model Calculator,

For the Engineer, Machinist, Manufacturer of Engine Work, Naval Architect, Miner, and Millwright. By OLIVER BYRNE, Compiler and Editor of the Dictionary of Machines, Mechanics, Engine Work and Engineering, and Author of various Mathematical and Mechanical Works. Illustrated by numerous engravings. Complete in one large volume, octavo, of nearly six hundred pages,..$4.50

The principal objects of this work are: to establish model calculations to guide practical men and students; to illustrate every practical rule and principle by numerical calculations, systematically arranged; to give information and data indispensable to those for whom it is intended, thus surpassing in value any other book of its character; to economize the labor of the practical man, and to render his every-day calculations easy and comprehensive. It will be found to be one of the most complete and valuable practical books ever published.

Cabinetmaker's and Upholsterer's Companion,

Comprising the Rudiments and Principles of Cabinetmaking and Upholstery, with Familiar Instructions, illustrated by Examples for attaining a proficiency in the Art of Drawing, as applicable to Cabinet Work; the processes of Veneering, Inlaying, and Buhl Work; the Art of Dyeing and Staining Wood, Bone, Tortoise Shell, etc. Directions for Lackering, Japanning, and Varnishing; to make French Polish; to prepare the best Glues, Cements, and Compositions, and a number of Receipts particularly useful for Workmen generally. By J. STOKES. In one volume, 12mo. With Illustrations,.......... $1.25

"A large amount of practical information, of great service to all concerned in those branches of business."

Campin. A Practical Treatise on Mechanical Engineering;

Comprising Metallurgy, Moulding, Casting, Forging, Tools, Workshop Machinery, Mechanical Manipulation,

Construction of Steam Boilers and remarks upon Furnaces used for Smoke Prevention; with a Chapter on Explosions. By R Armstrong, C. E., and John Bourne. Rules for Calculating the Change Wheels for Screws on a Turning Lathe, and for a Wheel-cutting Machine. By J. La Nicca. Management of Steel, including Forging, Hardening, Tempering, Annealing, Shrinking, and Expansion. And the Case-hardening of Iron. By G. Ede. 8vo. Illustrated with 29 plates and 100 wood engravings. 8vo........................$6.00

Colburn. 'The Locomotive Engine;

Including a Description of its Structure, Rules for Estimating its Capabilities, and Practical Observations on its Construction and Management. By ZERAH COLBURN. Illustrated. A new edition. 12mo,........................$1.25

"It is the most practical and generally useful work on the Steam Engine that we have seen."—*Boston Traveler.*"

Daguerreotypist and Photographer's Companion.

12mo., cloth, ...$1.25

Distiller (The Complete Practical).

By M. LAFAYETTE BYRN, M.D. With Illustrations. 12mo. $1.25

"So simplified. that it is adapted not only to the use of extensive Distillers, but for every farmer, or others who may want to engage in Distilling."—*Banner of the Union.*

Dussauce. Practical Treatise

ON THE FABRICATION OF MATCHES, GUN COTTON, AND FULMINATING POWDERS. By Prof. H. Dussauce. 12mo.,....$3.00

CONTENTS.— *Phosphorus.* — History of Phosphorus; Physical Properties; Chemical Properties; Natural State; Preparation of White Phosphorus; Amorphous Phosphorus, and Benoxide of Lead. *Matches.*—Preparation of Wooden Matches; Matches inflammable by rubbing, without noise; Common Lucifer Matches: Matches without Phosphorus; Candle Matches; Matches with Amorphous Phosphorus; Matches and Rubbers without Phosphorus. *Gun Cotton.*—Properties; Preparation; Paper Powder; use of Cotton and Paper Powders for Fulminating Primers, etc.; Preparation of Fulminating Primers, etc., etc.

Dussauce. Chemical Receipt Book:

A General Formulary for the Fabrication of Leading Chemicals, and their Application to the Arts, Manufac-

DYEING, CALICO PRINTING, COLORS, COTTON SPINNING, AND WOOLEN MANUFACTURE.

Baird. The American Cotton Spinner, and Manager's and Carder's Guide:

A Practical Treatise on Cotton Spinning; giving the Dimensions and Speed of Machinery, Draught and Twist Calculations, etc.; with Notices of recent Improvements: together with Rules and Examples for making changes in the sizes and numbers of Roving and Yarn. Compiled from the papers of the late Robert H. Baird. 12mo.................. ....$1.25

Capron De Dole. Dussauce. Blues and Carmines of Indigo:

A Practical Treatise on the Fabrication of every Commercial Product derived from Indigo. By Felicien Capron de Dole. Translated, with important additions, by Professor H. Dussauce. 12mo....................................$2.50

Chemistry Applied to Dyeing.

By James Napier, F. C. S. Illustrated. 12mo........$2.50

CONTENTS.—*General Properties of Matter.*—Heat, Light, Elements of Matter, Chemical Affinity. *Non-Metallic Substances.*—Oxygen, Hydrogen, Nitrogen, Chlorine, Sulphur, Selenium, Phosphorus, Iodine, Bromine, Fluorine, Silicum, Boron, Carbon. *Metallic Substances.*—General Properties of Metals, Potassium, Sodium, Lithium, Soap, Barium. Strontium, Calcium, Magnesium, Alminum, Manganese, Iron, Cobalt, Nickel, Zinc, Cadmium, Copper, Lead, Bismuth, Tin, Titanium, Chromium, Vanadium, Tungstenum or Wolfram, Molybdenum, Tellarium, Arsenic, Antimony, Uranium, Cerium, Mercury, Silver, Gold, Platinum, Palladium, Iridium, Osmium, Rhodium, Lanthanium. *Mordants.*—Red Spirits, Barwood Spirits, Plumb Spirits, Yellow Spirits, Nitrate of Iron, Acetate of Alumina, Black Iron Liquor, Iron and Tin for Royal Blues, Acetate of Copper. *Vegetable Matters used in Dyeing.*—Galls, Sumach, Catechu, Indigo, Logwood, Brazil-woods, Sandal-wood, Barwood, Camwood, Fustic, Young Fustic, Bark or Quercitron, Flavine, Weld or Wold, Turmeric, Persian Berries, Safflower, Madder, Munjeet, Annota, Alkanet Root, Archil. *Proposed New Vegetable Dyes.*—Sooranjee, Carajuru, Wongshy, Aloes, Pittacal, Barbary Root. *Animal Matters used in Dyeing.*—Cochineal, Lake or Lac, Kerms.

This will be found one of the most valuable books on the subject of dyeing, ever published in this country.

Dussauce. Treatise on the Coloring Matters Derived from Coal Tar;

tillation of Coal ar; with a Description of the most Important New Dyes now in use. By Professor H. Dussauce, Chemist. 12mo...$2.50

CONTENTS.—Historical Notice of the Art of Dyeing—Chemical Principles of the Art of Dyeing—Preliminary Preparation of Stuffs—Mordants—Dyeing—On the Coloring Matters produced by Coal Tar—Distillation of Coal Tar—History of Aniline—Properties of Aniline—Preparation of Aniline directly from Coal Tar—Artificial Preparation of Aniline—Preparation of Benzole—Properties of Benzole—Preparation of Nitro-Benzole—Transformation of Nitro-Benzole into Aniline, by means of Sulphide of Ammonium; by Nascent Hydrogen; by Acetate of Iron; and by Arsenite of Potash—Properties of the Bi-Nitro-Benzole—Aniline Purple—Violine—Roseine—Emeraldine—Bleu de Paris—Futschine, or Magenta—Coloring Matters obtained by other bases from Coal Tar—Nitroso-Phenyline—Di Nitro-Aniline—Nitro-Phenyline—Picric Acid—Rosolic Acid—Quinoline—Napthaline Colors—Chloroxynaphthalic and Perchloroxynapthalic Acids—Carminaphtha—Ninaphthalamine—Nitrosonaphthaline—Naphthamein—Tar Red—Azuline—Application of Coal Tar Colors to the Art of Dyeing and Calico Printing—Action of Light on Coloring Matters from Coal Tar—Latest Improvements in the Art of Dyeing—Chrysammic Acid—Molybdic and Picric Acids—Extract of Madder—Theory of the Fixation of Coloring Matters in Dyeing and Printing—Principles of the Action of the most important Mordants—Aluminous Mordants—Ferruginous Mordants—Stanniferous Mordants—Artificial Alizarin—Metallic Hyposulphites as Mordants—Dyer's Soap—Preparation of Indigo for Dyeing and Printing—Relative Value of Indigo—Chinese Green Murexide.

Dyer and Color-maker's Companion:

Containing upwards of two hundred Receipts for making Colors; on the most approved principles, for all the various styles and fabrics now in existence; with the Scouring Process, and plain Directions for Preparing, Washing-off, and Finishing the Goods. Second edition. In one volume, 12mo...$1.25

French Dyer, (The):

Comprising the Art of Dyeing in Woolen, Silk, Cotton, etc., etc. By M. M. Riffault, Vernaud, De Fontenelle, Thillaye, and Mallepeyre. (*In press.*)

Love. The Art of Dyeing, Cleaning, Scouring, and Finishing,

ON THE MOST APPROVED ENGLISH AND FRENCH METHODS; being Practical Instructions in Dyeing Silks, Woolens and Cottons, Feathers, Chips, Straw, etc., Scouring and Cleaning Bed and Window Curtains, Carpets, Rugs, etc., French and English Cleaning, any Color or Fabric of Silk, Satin, or Damask. By Thomas Love, a working Dyer and Scourer. In one volume, 12mo...............$3.00

ing, and Bleaching ;

Including Silken, Woolen, and Mixed Goods ; **Practical** and Theoretical. By Charles O'Neill. (*In press.*)

O'Neill. A Dictionary of Calico Printing and Dyeing.

By Charles O'Neill. (*In press.*)

Scott. The Practical Cotton-spinner and Manufacturer ;

OR, THE MANAGER AND OVERLOOKER'S COMPANION. This work contains a Comprehensive System of Calculations for Mill Gearing and Machinery, from the first Moving Power, through the different processes of Carding, Drawing, Slabbing, Roving, Spinning, and Weaving, adapted to American Machinery, Practice and Usages. Compendious Tables of Yarns and Reeds are added. Illustrated by large Working-Drawings of the most approved American Cotton Machinery. Complete in one volume, octavo...$5.00

This edition of Scott's Cotton-Spinner, by Oliver Byrne, is designed for the American Operative. It will be found intensely practical, and will be of the greatest possible value to the Manager, Overseer, and Workman.

Sellers. The Color-mixer.

By John Sellers, an Experienced Practical Workman. To which is added a CATECHISM OF CHEMISTRY. In one volume, 12mo..$2.50

Smith. The Dyer's Instructor ;

Comprising Practical Instructions in the Art of Dyeing Silk, Cotton, Wool and Worsted, and Woolen Goods, as Single and Two-colored Damasks, Moreens, Camlets, Lastings, Shot Cobourgs, Silk Striped Orleans, Plain Orleans, from White and Colored Warps, Merinos, Woolens, Yarns, etc.; containing nearly eight hundred Receipts. To which is added a Treatise on the Art of Padding, and the Printing of Silk Warps, Skeins and Handkerchiefs, and the various Mordants and Colors for the different styles of such work. By David Smith, Pattern Dyer. A new edition, in one volume, 12mo.......................$3.00

CONTENTS.—Wool Dyeing, 60 receipts—Cotton Dyeing, 68 receipts—Silk Dyeing, 60 receipts—Woolen Yarn Dyeing, 59 receipts—Worsted Yarn Dyeing, 51 receipts—Woolen Dyeing, 52 receipts—Damask Dyeing, 40 receipts—Moreen Dyeing, 88 receipts—Two-Colored Damask Dyeing, 21 receipts—Camlet Dyeing, 23 receipts—Lasting Dyeing, 28 receipts—Shot Cobourg Dyeing, 18 receipts—Silk Striped Orleans, from Black, White, and Colored Warps, 23 receipts—Colored Orleans, from Black Warps, 15 receipts—Colored Orleans and Cobourgs, from White Warps, 27 receipts—Colored Merinos, 41 receipts—Woolen Shawl Dyeing, 15 receipts—Padding, 42 receipts—Silk Warp, Skein, and Handkerchief Printing, 62 receipts—Nature and Use of Dyewares, including Alum, Annotta, Archil, Ammonia, Argol, Super Argol, Camwood, Catechu, Cochineal, Chrome, or Bichromate of Potash, Cudbear, Chemic, or Sulphate of Indigo, French Berry, or Persian Berry, Fustic or Young Fustic, Galls, Indigo, Kermes or Lac Dye, Logwood, Madder, Nitric Acid or Aqua Fortis, Nitrates, Oxalic Tin, Peachwood, Prussiate of Potash, Quercitron Bark, Safflower, Saunders or Red Sandal, Sapan Wood, Sumach, Turmeric, Examination of Water by Tests, etc., etc.

Ulrich. Dussauce. A Complete Treatise

ON THE ART OF DYEING COTTON AND WOOL, AS PRACTISED IN PARIS, ROUEN, MULHOUSE AND GERMANY. From the French of M. Louis Ulrich, a Practical Dyer in the principal Manufactories of Paris, Rouen, Mulhouse, etc., etc.; to which are added the most important Receipts for Dyeing Wool, as practised in the Manufacture Imperiale des Gobelins, Paris. By Professor H. Dussauce. 12mo..$3.00

CONTENTS.—

Rouen Dyes,	106	Receipts.
Alsace "	225	"
German "	109	"
Mulhouse "	72	"
Parisian "	56	"
Gobelins "	100	"

In all nearly 700 Receipts.

Easton. A Practical Treatise on Street or Horse-power Railways;

Their Location, Construction and Management; with

tive Advantages over the Omnibus System, and Inquiries as to their Value for Investment; including Copies of Municipal Ordinances relating thereto. By Alexander Easton, C. E. Illustrated by twenty-three plates, 8vo., cloth..$2.00

Examinations of Drugs, Medicines, Chemicals, etc.,

As to their Purity and Adulterations. By C. H. Peirce, M. D. 12mo., cloth..$2.50

Fisher's Photogenic Manipulation.

16mo., cloth.. 62

Gas and Ventilation;

A Practical Treatise on Gas and Ventilation. By E. E. Perkins. 12mo., cloth.......................................$1.00

Gilbart. A Practical Treatise on Banking.

By James William Gilbart, F. R. S. A new enlarged and improved edition. Edited by J. Smith Homans, editor of "Banker's Magazine." To which is added "Money," by H. C. Carey. 8vo...$3.50

Gregory's Mathematics for Practical Men;

Adapted to the Pursuits of Surveyors, Architects, Mechanics and Civil Engineers. 8vo., plates, cloth...$2.25

Hardwich. A Manual of Photographic Chemistry;

Including the practice of the Collodion Process. By J. F. Hardwich. (*In press.*)

Hay. The Interior Decorator;

The Laws of Harmonious Coloring adapted to Interior Decorations; with a Practical Treatise on House Painting. By D. R. Hay, House Painter and Decorator. Il-

Or, a Guide to Inventors, and a Book of Reference for Judges, Lawyers, Magistrates, and others. By J. G. Moore. 12mo., cloth..$1.25

Jervis. Railway Property. A Treatise

On the Construction and Management of Railways; designed to afford useful knowledge, in the popular style, to the holders of this class of property; as well as Railway Managers, Officers and Agents. By John B. Jervis, late Chief Engineer of the Hudson River Railroad, Croton Aqueduct, etc. One volume, 12mo., cloth........$2.00

CONTENTS. — Preface — Introduction. *Construction.* — Introductory—Land and Land Damages—Location of Line—Method of Business—Grading—Bridges and Culverts—Road Crossings—Ballasting Track—Cross Sleepers—Chairs and Spikes—Rails—Station Buildings—Locomotives, Coaches and Cars. *Operating.*—Introductory—Freight—Passengers—Engine Drivers—Repairs to Track—Repairs of Machinery—Civil Engineer—Superintendent—Supplies of Material—Receipts—Disbursements — Statistics — Running Trains — Competition — Financial Management—General Remarks.

Johnson. The Coal Trade of British America;

With Researches on the Characters and Practical Values of American and Foreign Coals. By Walter R. Johnson, Civil and Mining Engineer and Chemist. 8vo........$2.00

This volume contains the results of the experiments made for the Navy Department, upon which their Coal contracts are now based.

Johnston. Instructions for the Analysis of Soils, Limestones and Manures.

By J. F. W. Johnston. 12mo................................. 38

Larkin. The Practical Brass and Iron Founder's Guide;

A Concise Treatise on the Art of Brass Founding, Moulding, etc. By James Larkin. 12mo., cloth.............$1.25

Leslie's (Miss) Complete Cookery;

Directions for Cookery in its Various Branches. By Miss Leslie. 58th thousand. Thoroughly revised; with the addition of New Receipts. In one volume, 12mo., half bound, or in sheep..$1.25

Leslie's (Miss) Ladies' House Book;

A Manual of Domestic Economy. 20th revised edition. 12mo., sheep $1.25

Leslie's (Miss) Two Hundred Receipts in French Cookery.

Cloth, 12mo.. 25

Lieber. Assayer's Guide;

Or, Practical Directions to Assayers, Miners and Smelters, for the Tests and Assays, by Heat and by Wet Processes, of the Ores of· all the principal Metals, and of Gold and Silver Coins and Alloys. By Oscar M. Lieber, late Geologist to the State of Mississippi. 12mo. With illustrations $1.25

"Among the indispensable works for this purpose, is this little guide."—*Artizan.*

Lowig. Principles of Organic and Physiological Chemistry.

By Dr. Carl Löwig, Doctor of Medicine and Philosophy; Ordinary Professor of Chemistry in the University of Zürich; Author of "Chemie des Organischen Verbindungen." Translated by Daniel Breed, M. D., of the U. S. Patent Office; late of the Laboratory of Liebig and Lowig. 8vo., sheep...$3.50

Marble Worker's Manual;

Containing Practical Information respecting Marbles in general, their Cutting, Working and Polishing, Veneering, etc., etc. 12mo., cloth.................................$1.25

Miles. A Plain Treatise on Horse-shoeing.

With Illustrations. By William Miles, Author of "The Horse's Foot."..$1.00

at the Royal Naval College, Portsmouth, and Thomas Brown, Assoc. Inst. C. E. Chief Engineer R. N. attached to the Royal Naval College. Authors of "Questions Connected with the Marine Steam-Engine," and the "Indicator and Dynamometer." With Numerous Illustrations. In one Volume, 8vo.............. ....$5.00

CONTENTS.—Introductory Chapter, The Boiler, The Engine, Getting up Steam, Duties to Machinery when under Steam, Duties to Engine, &c., on arriving in harbor, Miscellaneous, Appendix.

Main & Brown. Questions on Subjects Connected with the Marine-Steam Engine,

And Examination Papers ; with Hints for their Solution. By Thomas J. Main, Professor of Mathematics Royal Naval College, and Thomas Brown, Chief Engineer R. N. 12mo., cloth...... ....$1.50

Main & Brown. The Indicator and Dynamometer,

With their Practical Applications to the Steam Engine. By Thomas J. Main and Thomas Brown. With Illustrations. 8vo., cloth....... ....$1.50

Morfit. A Treatise on Chemistry

APPLIED TO THE MANUFACTURE OF SOAP AND CANDLES ; being a Thorough Exposition, in all their Minutiæ, of the principles and Practice of the Trade, based upon the most recent Discoveries in Science and Art. By Campbell Morfit, Professor of Analytical and Applied Chemistry in the University of Maryland. A new and improved edition. Illustrated with 260 Engravings on Wood. Complete in one volume, large 8vo.................................$7.50

CONTENTS.—CHAPTER I. The History of the Art and its Relations to Science—II. Chemical Combination—III. Alkalies and Alkaline Earths—IV. Alkalimentary—V. Acids—VI. Origin and Composition of Fatty Matters—VII. Saponifiable Fats—Vegetable Fats—Animal Fats—Waxes—VIII. Action of Heat and Mineral Acids of Fatty Matters—IX. Volatile or Essential Oils, and Resins—X. The Proximate Principles of Fats—Their Composition and Properties—Basic Constituents of Fats—XI. Theory of Saponification—XII. Utensils Requisite for a Soap Factory—XIII. Preparatory Manipulations in the Process of Making Soap—Preparation of the Lyes—XIV. Hard

Soaps—XV. Soft Soaps—XVI. Soaps by the Cold Process—XVII. Sili·cated Soaps—XVIII. Toilet Soaps—XIX. Patent Soaps—XX. Fraud and Adulterations in the Manufacture of Soap—XXI. Candles—XXII. Illumination—XXIII. Philosophy of Flame—XXIV. Raw Material for Candles—Purification and Bleaching of Suet—XXV. Wicks—XXVI. Dipped Candles—XXVII. Moulded Candles—XXVIII. Stearin Candles—XXIX. Stearic Acid Candles—"Star" or "Adamantine" Candles—Saponification by Lime—Saponification by Lime and Sulphurous Acid—Saponification by Sulphuric Acid—Saponification by the combined action of Heat, Pressure and Steam—XXX. Spermaceti Candles—XXXI. Wax Candles—XXXII. Composite Candles—XXXIII. Paraffin—XXXIV. Patent Candles—XXXV. Hydrometers and Thermometers.

Mortimer. Pyrotechnist's Companion;

Or, a Familiar System of Fire-works. By G. W. Mortimer. Illustrated by numerous Engravings. 12mo $1.25

Napier. Manual of Electro-Metallurgy;

Including the Application of the Art to Manufacturing Processes. By James Napier. From the second London edition, revised and enlarged. Illustrated by Engravings. In one volume, 12mo...$1.50

Napier's Electro-Metallurgy is generally regarded as the very best Practical Treatise on the Subject in the English Language.

CONTENTS.—History of the Art of Electro-Metallurgy—Description of Galvanic Batteries, and their respective Peculiarities—Electrotype Processes—Miscellaneous Applications of the Process of Coating with Copper — Bronzing — Decomposition of Metals upon one another—Electro-Plating—Electro-Gilding—Results of Experiments on the Deposition of other Metals as Coatings, Theoretical Observations.

Norris's Hand-book for Locomotive Engineers and Machinists;

Comprising the Calculations for Constructing Locomotives, Manner of setting Valves, etc., etc. By Septimus Norris, Civil and Mechanical Engineer. In one volume, 12mo., with Illustrations..$2.00

" With pleasure do we meet with such a work as Messrs. Norris and Baird have given us."—*Artizan.*
" In this work he has given us what are called 'the secrets of the business,' in the rules to construct locomotives, in order that the million should be learned in all things."—*Scientific American.*

Nystrom. A Treatise on Screw-Propellers and their Steam-Engines;

With Practical Rules and Examples by which to Calculate and Construct the same for any description of Ves-

Overman. The Manufacture of Iron in all its Various Branches;

To which is added an Essay on the Manufacture of Steel. By Frederick Overman, Mining Engineer. With one hundred and fifty Wood Engravings. Third edition. In one volume, octavo, five hundred pages........ ....$7.50

" We have now to announce the appearance of another valuable work on the subject, which, in our humble opinion, supplies any deficiency which late improvements and discoveries may have caused, from the lapse of time since the date of ' Mushet' and ' Schrivenor.' It is the production of one of our Trans-Atlantic brethren, Mr. Frederick Overman, Mining Engineer ; and we do not hesitate to set it down as a work of great importance to all connected with the iron interests ; one which, while it is sufficiently technological fully to explain chemical analysis, and the various phenomena of iron under different circumstances, to the satisfaction of the most fastidious, is written in that clear and comprehensive style as to be available to the capacity of the humblest mind, and consequently will be of much advantage to those works where the proprietors may see the desirability of placing it in the hands of their operatives."—*London Mining Journal.*

Painter, Gilder and Varnisher's Companion;

Containing Rules and Regulations in every thing relating to the Arts of Painting, Gilding, Varnishing and Glass Staining ; with numerous useful and valuable Receipts ; Tests for the detection of Adulterations in Oils and Colors ; and a statement of the Diseases and Accidents to which Painters, Gilders and Varnishers are particularly liable, with the simplest methods of Prevention and Remedy. Eighth edition. To which are added Complete Instructions in Graining, Marbling, Sign Writing, and Gilding on Glass. 12mo., cloth........ .... $1.25

Paper-Hanger's (The) Companion;

In which the Practical Operations of the Trade are systematically laid down ; with copious Directions Preparatory to Papering ; Preventions against the effect of Damp in Walls ; the various Cements and Pastes adapted to the several purposes of the Trade ; Observations and Directions for the Panelling and Ornamenting of Rooms, etc., etc. By James Arrowsmith. In one volume 12mo ....,..... .... $1.25

Practical (The) Surveyor's Guide;

out the aid of a Teacher. By Andrew Duncan, Land
Surveyor and Civil Engineer. 12mo................ $1.25

Having had an experience as a Practical Surveyor, etc., of thirty
years, it is believed that the author of this volume possesses a thorough
knowledge of the wants of the profession ; and never having met with
any work sufficiently concise and instructive in the several details
necessary for the proper qualification of the Surveyor, it has been his
object to supply that want. Among other important matters in the
book, will be found the following :

Instructions in levelling and profiling, with a new and speedy plan
of setting grades on rail and plank roads—the method of inflecting
curves—the description and design of a new instrument, whereby distances are found at once, without any calculation—a new method of
surveying any tract of land by measuring one line through it—a geo-
metrical method of correcting surveys taken with the compass, to fit
them for calculation—a short method of finding the angles from the
courses, and *vice versa*—the method of surveying with the compass
through any mine or iron works, and to correct the deflections of the
needle by attraction—description of an instrument by the help of
which any one may measure a map by inspection, without calculation
—a new and short method of calculation, wherein fewer figures are
used—the method of correcting the diurnal variation of the needle
—various methods of plotting and embellishing maps—the most correct method of laying off plots with the pole, etc.—description of a
new compass contrived by the author, etc., etc

Railroad Engineer's Pocket Companion for the Field.

By W. Griswold. 12mo., tucks......................$1.25

Regnault. Elements of Chemistry.

By M. V. Regnault. Translated from the French by T.
Forrest Betton, M.D., and edited, with notes, by James
C. Booth, Melter and Refiner U. S. Mint, and William L.
Faber, Metallurgist and Mining Engineer. Illustrated by
nearly 700 wood engravings. Comprising nearly 1,500
pages. In two volumes, 8vo., cloth............ ....$10.00

Rural Chemistry;

An Elementary Introduction to the Study of the Science,
in its relation to Agriculture and the Arts of Life. By
Edward Solly, Professor of Chemistry in the Horticul-
tural Society of London. From the third improved London edition. 12mo...$1.50

Shunk. A Practical Treatise

On Railway Curves, and Location for Young Engineers.
B Wm. F. Shunk Civil En ineer. 12mo............ 1.06

perties of Metals for Cannon. With a Description of the Machines for Testing Metals, and of the Classification of Cannon in service. By Officers of the Ordnance Department U. S. Army. By authority of the Secretary of War. Illustrated by 25 large steel plates. In one volume, quarto..$10.00

The best Treatise on Cast-iron extant.

Tables Showing the Weight

Of Round, Square and Flat Bar Iron, Steel, etc., by Measurement. Cloth... 50

Taylor. Statistics of Coal;

Including Mineral Bituminous Substances employed in Arts and Manufactures; with their Geographical, Geological and Commercial Distribution, and Amount of Production and Consumption on the American Continent. With Incidental Statistics of the Iron Manufacture. By R. C. Taylor. Second edition, revised by S. S. Haldeman. Illustrated by five Maps and many Wood Engravings. 8vo., cloth..$6.00

Templeton. The Practical Examinator on Steam and the Steam Engine;

With Instructive References relative thereto, arranged for the use of Engineers, Students, and others. By Wm. Templeton, Engineer. 12mo...........................$1.25

This work was originally written for the author's private use. He was prevailed upon by various Engineers, who had seen the notes, to consent to its publication, from their eager expression of belief that it would be equally useful to them as it had been to himself.

Tin and Sheet Iron Worker's Instructor;

Comprising complete Descriptions of the necessary Patterns and Machinery, and the Processes of Calculating Dimensions, Cutting, Joining, Raising, Soldering, etc. etc. With numerous Illustrations. $2.50

atise (A) on a Box of Instruments,

And the Slide Rule; with the Theory of Trigonometry

A volume of inestimable value to Engineers, Gaugers, Students, and others.

Turnbull. The Electro-Magnetic Telegraph;

With an Historical Account of its Rise, Progress, and Present Condition. Also, Practical Suggestions in regard to Insulation and Protection from the Effects of Lightning. Together with an Appendix containing several important Telegraphic Devices and Laws. By Lawrence Turnbull, M. D., Lecturer on Technical Chemistry at the Franklin. Institute. Second edition. Revised and improved. Illustrated by numerous Engravings. 8vo..$2.50

Turner's (The) Companion;

Containing Instruction in Concentric, Elliptic and Eccentric Turning; also various Steel Plates of Chucks, Tools and Instruments; and Directions for Using the Eccentric Cutter, Drill, Vertical Cutter and Rest; with Patterns and Instructions for working them. 12mo., cloth.. $1.25

Weatherley (Henry). Treatise on the Art of Boiling Sugar, Crystallizing, Lozenge-making, Comfits, Gum Goods,

12mo........ ....$2.00

Williams. On Heat and Steam:

Embracing New Views of Vaporization, Condensation, and Expansion. By Charles Wye Williams. Illustrated. 8vo............ .... $3.50

SOCIAL SCIENCE.

THE WORKS OF HENRY C. CAREY.

"I challenge the production from among the writers on political economy of a more learned, philosophical, and convincing speculator on that theme, than my distinguished fellow-citizen, Henry C. Carey. The works he has published in support of the protective policy, are remarkable for profound research, extensive range of inquiry, rare logical acumen, and a consummate knowledge of history."—*Speech of Hon. Edward Joy Morris, in the House of Representatives of the United States, February 2, 1859.*

"Henry C. Carey, the best known and ablest economist of North America. * * * * In Europe he is principally known by his striking and original attacks, based upon the peculiar advantages of American experience, on some of the principal doctrines, especially Malthus' 'Theory of Population' and Ricardo's teachings. His views have been largely adopted and thoroughly discussed in Europe."— "*The German Political Lexicon*," *Edited by Bluntschli and Brater. Leipsic,* 1858.

"We believe that your labors mark an era in the science of political economy. To your researches and lucid arguments are we indebted for the explosion of the absurdities of Malthus, Say, and Ricardo, in regard to the inability of the earth to meet the demands of a growing population. American industry owes you a debt which cannot be repaid, and which it will ever be proud to acknowledge.—*From a Letter of Hon. George W. Scranton, M. C., Hon. William Jessup, and over sixty influential citizens of Luzerne County, Pennsylvania, to Henry C. Carey, April* 3, 1859.

Financial Crises;

Their Causes and Effects. 8vo., paper...................... 25

French and American Tariffs,

Compared in a Series of Letters addressed to Mons. M. Chevalier. 8vo., paper.. 25

Harmony (The) of Interests;

Agricultural, Manufacturing and Commercial. 8vo., paper... 75
Cloth. $1.50

"We can safely recommend this remarkable work to all who wish to investigate the causes of the progress or decline of industrial communities."—*Blackwood's Magazine.*

Letters to the President of the United States.

8vo., Paper... 50

Miscellaneous Works;

Comprising "Harmony of Interests," "Money," "Letters to the President," "French and American Tariffs," and "Financial Crises." One volume, 8vo. $3.00

Money; A Lecture

Before the New York Geographical and Statistical Society. 8vo. paper... 25

Past (The), the Present, and the Future.

8vo.......... ....$2.50
12mo.......... .... $1.50

" Full of important facts bearing on topics that are now agitating all Europe. * * * These quotations will only whet the appetite of the scientific reader to devour the whole work. It is a book full of valuable information."—*Economist.*

" Decidedly a book to be read by all who take an interest in the progress of social science."—*Spectator.*

"A Southern man myself, never given to tariff doctrines, I confess to have been convinced by his reasoning, and, thank Heaven, have not now to learn the difference between dogged obstinacy and consistency. ' Ye gods, give us but light !' should be the motto of every inquirer after truth, but for far different and better purposes than that which prompted the exclamation."—*The late John S. Skinner.*

" A volume of extensive information, deep thought, high intelligence, and moreover of material utility."—*London Morning Advertiser.*

" Emanating from an active intellect, remarkable for distinct views and sincere convictions."—*Britannia.*

" 'The Past, Present, and Future,' is a vast summary of progressive philosophy, wherein he demonstrates the benefit of political economy in the onward progress of mankind, which, ruled and directed by overwhelming influences of an exterior nature, advances little by little, until these exterior influences are rendered subservient in their turn, to increase as much as possible the extent of their wealth and riches " —*Dictionnaire Universel des Contemporains. Par G. Vapereau. Paris,* 1858.

Principles of Social Science.

Three volumes, 8vo., cloth.......... ....$10.00

CONTENTS.—Volume I. Of Science and its Methods—Of Man, the Subject of Social Science—Of Increase in the Numbers of Mankind —Of the Occupation of the Earth—Of Value—Of Wealth—Of the Formation of Society—Of Appropriation—Of Changes of Matter in Place —Of M hanical and Chemical Changes in the Forms of Matter. Volume II. Of Vital Changes in the Form of Matter—Of the Instrument of Association. Volume III. Of Production and Consumption—Of Accumulation—Of Circulation—Of Distribution—Of Concentration and Centralization—Of Competition—Of Population—Of Food and Population—Of Colonization—Of the Malthusian Theory—Of Commerce—Of the Societary Organization—Of Social Science.

" I have no desire here to reproach Mr. Malthus with the extreme lightness of his scientific baggage. In his day, biology, animal and vegetable chemistry, the relations of the various portions of the human organism, etc. etc., had made but little progress, and it is to the general ignorance in reference to these questions that we must, as I think, look for explanation of the fact that he should, with so much confidence, in reference to so very grave a subject, have ventured to suggest a formula so arbitrary in its character, and one whose hollowness becomes now so clearly manifest. Mr. Carey's advantage over him, both as to facts and logic, is certainly due in great part to the progress that has since been made in all the sciences connected with life ; but then, how admirably has he profited of them ! How entirely is he au courant of all these branches of knowledge which, whether

22

directly or indirectly, bear upon his subject! With what skill does he ask of each and every of them all that it can be made to furnish, whether of facts or arguments! With what elevated views, and what amplitude of means, does he go forward in his work! Above all, how thorough in his scientific caution! Accumulating inductions and presenting for consideration facts the most undoubted and proba bilities of the highest kind, he yet affirms nothing, contenting himself with showing that his opponent had no good reason for affirming the nature of the progression, nor the time of duplication, nor the gene- ralization which takes the facts of an individual case and deduces from them a law for every race, every climate, every civilization, every condition, moral or physical, permanent and transient, healthy or unhealthy, of the various populations of the many coun- tries of the world. Then, having reduced the theory to the level of a mere hypothesis, he crushes it to atoms under the weight of facts."— *M. De Fontenay in the "Journal des Economistes." Paris, September,* 1862.

" This book is so abundantly full of notices, facts, comparisons, cal- culations, and arguments, that too much would be lost by laying a part of it before the eye of the reader. The work is vast and severe in its conception and aim, and is far removed from the common run of the books on similar subjects."—*Il Mondo Letterario, Turin.*

" In political economy, America is represented by one of the strongest and most original writers of the age, Henry C. Carey, of Philadelphia. * * * * * * * * * * " His theory of Rents is regarded as a complete demonstration that the popular views derived from Ricardo are erroneous; and on the subject of Protection, he is generally confessed to be the master- thinker of his country."—*Westminster Review.*

" Both in America and on the Continent, Mr. Henry Carey has ac- quired a great name as a political economist. * * * * * " His refutation of Malthus and Ricardo we consider most triumph- ant."—*London Critic.*

" Mr. Carey began his publication of Principles twenty years ago ; he is certainly a mature and deliberate writer. More than this, he is readable : his pages swarm with illustrative facts and with American instances. * * * * * * * * * " We are in great charity with books which, like Mr. Carey's, theo- rize with excessive boldness, when the author, as does Mr. Carey, possesses information and reasoning power."—*London Athenæum.*

" Those who would fight against the insatiate greed and unscrupu- lous misrepresentations of the Manchester school, which we have fre- quently exposed, without any of their organs having ever dared to make reply, will find in this and Mr. Carey's other works an immense store of arms and ammunition. * * * * * * " An author who has, among the political economists of Germany and France, numerous readers, is worth attentive perusal in Eng- land."—*London Statesman.*

" Of all the varied answers to the old cry of human nature, 'Who will show us any good?' none are more sententious than Mr. Carey's. He says to Kings, Presidents, and People, 'Keep the nation at work, and the greater the variety of employments the better.' He is seek- ing and elucidating the great radical laws of matter as regards man. He is at once the apostle and evangelist of temporal righteousness." —*National Intelligencer.*

" A work which we believe to be the greatest ever written by an American, and one which will in future ages be pointed out as the most successful effort of its time to form the great *scientia scientiarum*." —*Philadelphia Evening Bulletin.*

The Slave Trade, Domestic and Foreign;

Why it Exists, and How it may be Extinguished. 12mo., cloth..$1.50

CONTENTS.—The Wide Extent of Slavery—Of Slavery in the British Colonies—Of Slavery in the United States—Of Emancipation in the British Colonies—How Man passes from Poverty and Slavery toward Wealth and Freedom—How Wealth tends to Increase—How Labor acquires Value and Man becomes Free—How Man passes from Wealth and Freedom toward Poverty and Slavery—How Slavery grew, and How it is now maintained in the West Indies—How Slavery grew, and is maintained in the United States—How Slavery grows in Portugal and Turkey—How Slavery grows in India—How Slavery grows in Ireland and Scotland—How Slavery grows in England—How can Slavery be extinguished?—How Freedom grows in Northern Germany—How Freedom grows in Russia—How Freedom grows in Denmark—How Freedom grows in Spain and Belgium—Of the Duty of the People of the United States—Of the Duty of the People of England.

" As a philosophical writer, Mr. Carey is remarkable for the union of comprehensive generalizations with a copious induction of facts. His research of principles never leads him to the neglect of details; nor is his accumulation of instances ever at the expense of universal truth. He is, doubtless, intent on the investigation of laws, as the appropriate aim of science, but no passion for theory seduces him into the region of pure speculation. His mind is no less historical than philosophical, and had he not chosen the severer branch in which his studies have borne such excellent fruit, he would have attained an eminent rank among the historians from whom the literature of our country has received such signal illustration."—*New York Tribune.*

French Politico-Economic Controversy,

Between the Supporters of the Doctrines of CAREY and of those of RICARDO and MALTHUS. By MM. De Fontenay, Dupuit, Baudrillart, and others. Translated from the "Journal des Economistes," 1862–63. (*In press.*)

Protection of Home Labor and Home Productions

Necessary to the Prosperity of the American Farmer. By H. C. Baird. Paper.. 13

Smith. A Manual of Political Economy.

By E. Peshine Smith. 12mo., cloth.......................$1.25